Isaiah

K.W. Bow

Copyright 2016 by Kenneth W. Bow, Vaughn Reece,
Scott Hall and Bart Adkins
The book authors retain copyright to
their contributions to this book.

Published 2016.
Printed in the United States of America.

All rights reserved.

No portion of this book may be reproduced, stored in a retrieval system, or transmitted in any form or by any means – electronic, mechanical, photocopy, recording, scanning, or other – except for brief quotations in critical reviews or articles, without the prior written permission of the author.

ISBN 978-1-946234-00-1

Front cover design by Mark Gauthier.

This book was published by BookCrafters,
Parker, Colorado.
bookcrafterscolorado@gmail.com

This book may be ordered from
www.bookcrafters.net and other online bookstores.

Foreword

Thank you reader for selecting my book. There are many choices of books and we all have a limited window of time to read. I appreciate you purchasing my product. It is a humbling thing to know someone would choose to purchase, and then read your work. I do not take it as a small matter. By purchasing and reading a book, the reader and the author form a certain bond as they travel a road together for a short time. It is especially rewarding when the two agree on the content. It is my hope you can find inspiration and life challenges in the pages of this small booklet.

From the days of my high school years I have found the Bible fascinating. I have travelled to Israel on two occasions to learn more about the land and culture of the Bible. I worked on an archaeological dig and lived on a Kibbutz to better inform myself of how to understand this book from God. I have read it from cover to cover over twenty times, and it is still as exciting to me as it ever was.

The Bible is a magnificent journey and experience. It is ever a delight. In it you will travel to distant lands and meet some of the most incredible people of history.

It will introduce you to kings and peasants. You will walk the palace halls of castles and the open fields of the countryside. You will meet the famous and be introduced to people whose name we will never know. You will read some of the greatest love stories ever told and you will see the dark side of man as the evil manifests itself in heinous ways. Every emotion of man is highlighted at some time. You will see greed and avarice and murderous covetousness. You will also see the greatest examples of love and sacrifice that mankind has ever contributed. For indeed the Bible is the story of man. It is the whole story, and nothing is left out or omitted. It is the ultimate mirror of life.

When we invest time in the Bible we indulge a bit of the eternal. The Bible will never pass away, even in the eons of the future. If you have read it sincerely then my hope is this small work will intensify your understanding and enjoyment a little more. It is the grandest journey we can make while in this life. Thank you for sharing a portion of your life journey with me.

In this volume I include the commentary by other men who worked on Isaiah. I wrote the commentary for chapters 1-39. Vaughn Reece wrote the commentary for chapters 40-46. Scott Hall wrote the commentary for chapters 47-56. Bart Adkins wrote the commentary for chapters 57-66. I am proud to attach my name along with these outstanding Bible expositors.

Kenneth Bow

Introduction

In the eighth century BC while Homer was writing the Iliad and the Odyssey, and Lao Tzu was writing the Tao de Ching, Isaiah wrote the book that bears his name.

The prophet Isaiah was a giant of Jewish history. He is considered the Shakespeare of Hebrew literature. The New Testament quotes him more than all the other prophets added together. Ironically he is quoted 66 times, the same number of chapters in his book. All other prophets combined are quoted 33 times. No author in the Bible can match his eloquence and mastery of style and imagery.

He lived midway through the founding of the nation and its final destruction. He lived on the border between the Northern and Southern kingdom. He was one of the prophets who observed first-hand the fall and captivity of the Northern Kingdom of Israel. He preached for 64 years.

The Rabbis say that he was first cousin to King Uzziah. Isaiah's father, and Uzziah's father, were brothers. This would mean he was of royal lineage, and familiar with the palace and court life. He certainly was the confidant and advisor to at least 5 kings. He is a descendant of Judah and Tamar in the book of Genesis.

Isaiah was not a "yes" man to these kings. He stood against the popular tide of optimism. His name meant "The Lord saves." He warned Kings repeatedly that to depend on military power or wealth or alliances or anything but God would bring disaster.

Isaiah outlived four of the kings he advised, but finally offended one King beyond the King's tolerance. Manasseh is said to have placed Isaiah between two planks and had him sawed in half. Thus ending the life of one of Israel's greatest heroes. Some Rabbi's believe Isaiah hid in a cedar tree to escape Manasseh, who cut the tree in two, and also cut Isaiah in two.

Isaiah's writings are about the nature of God. It is a collection of many messages on many subjects.

His writings break down like this:

- Chapters 1-12 warnings to Judah during their prosperous days
- Chapters 13-23 messages to surrounding nations
- Chapters 24-35 earth's future and the imminent invasion of Assyria
- Chapters 36-39 an interlude telling of crisis Judah faced
- Chapters 40-48 prophesies 200 years into the future. (Babylon)
- Chapters 49-55 The nation's final deliverance through the suffering servant
- Chapters 56-66 warnings to Judah and a view of the future

These are quick bullet references to Isaiah:

- Began preaching before he was 20 years old
- A contemporary of Amos and Hosea
- Born during Uzziah's reign
- Called in the year Uzziah died
- Saw the Glory of Jeroboam II (Israel)
- Observed the fall of Israel in 721 BC
- Influenced Hezekiah
- Foretold the rise of Babylon
- Killed by Manasseh
- His book a mini Bible (66 chapter, 39,27)
- Proclaims the coming Messiah
- Quoted more in New Testament than all other prophets combined, (66 times vs. 33 times)
- Shakespeare of Hebrew literature
- First cousin to Uzziah
- Giant of Jewish history
- Lived exactly in the middle of the founding of the nation and its destruction
- His name means "the Lord saves"
- Prophesied during 5 kings
- Wrote same time as the Iliad and the Odyssey and Tao de Ching
- Looks into the nature of God
- He was Hezekiah's "song in the night"
- He preached for 64 years until he was almost 84 years old
- He was a 13 year old boy when his father Ahaz became King

His supreme contribution was his fore telling Messiah is coming. The nation hung onto this thread of hope until Jesus arrived. It helped keep them through the 400 silent years of despair. When the New Testament opens they are on point looking for Messiah.

Because he looks into the nature of God, He is our "One God" preacher. Verses like, 9.6, 7.14, 43.10-11, 44.6, 44.8, 45.15, as well as chapters 12, 35, and 53, are favorite one God passages. When an Apostolic preacher preaches on Oneness, he invariably visits the book of Isaiah.

When Assyria threatened the nation, after conquering 200 walled cities and leading away 200,000 captives from the northern nation, it was Isaiah who stayed calm while Hezekiah panicked. Isaiah was the song in the night with a word from the Lord. The next morning 185,000 Assyrians lay dead, Judah was saved, and Isaiah was right.

Isaiah had heard from God and the Angel of the Lord went through the camp of Assyria and slew 185,000 men while Israel slept and never lifted a finger.

The Devil was not alone in using Giants to do great exploits. God answered with some Giants of his own.

Of these, none stands taller than Isaiah.

Isaiah's book is a book of variety; it is very eclectic, with a variety of tone, style, thought and historical background.

The picture is of a man who loved his people, but was unbending in his nature, and loved his God most of all.

Chapter 1

1.1 1 The vision of Isaiah the son of Amoz, which he saw concerning Judah and Jerusalem in the days of Uzziah, Jotham, Ahaz, and Hezekiah, kings of Judah.

1.1 The reign of these five kings was from 754 until 695 BC. This would mean Isaiah would prophecy approximately 64 years, as he was killed during the reign of Manasseh.

1.2-31 Hear, O heavens, and give ear, O earth: for the Lord hath spoken, I have nourished and brought up children, and they have rebelled against me. 3 The ox knoweth his owner, and the ass his master's crib: but Israel doth not know, my people doth not consider. 4 Ah sinful nation, a people laden with iniquity, a seed of evildoers, children that are corrupters: they have forsaken the Lord, they have provoked the Holy One of Israel unto anger, they are gone away backward. 5 Why should ye be stricken any more? ye will revolt more and more: the whole head is sick, and the whole heart faint. 6 From the sole of the foot even unto the head there is no soundness in it; but wounds, and bruises, and putrifying sores: they have not been closed, neither bound up, neither mollified

with ointment. 7 Your country is desolate, your cities are burned with fire: your land, strangers devour it in your presence, and it is desolate, as overthrown by strangers. 8 And the daughter of Zion is left as a cottage in a vineyard, as a lodge in a garden of cucumbers, as a besieged city. 9 Except the Lord of hosts had left unto us a very small remnant, we should have been as Sodom, and we should have been like unto Gomorrah. 10 Hear the word of the Lord, ye rulers of Sodom; give ear unto the law of our God, ye people of Gomorrah. 11 To what purpose is the multitude of your sacrifices unto me? saith the Lord: I am full of the burnt offerings of rams, and the fat of fed beasts; and I delight not in the blood of bullocks, or of lambs, or of he goats. 12 When ye come to appear before me, who hath required this at your hand, to tread my courts? 13 Bring no more vain oblations; incense is an abomination unto me; the new moons and sabbaths, the calling of assemblies, I cannot away with; it is iniquity, even the solemn meeting. 14 Your new moons and your appointed feasts my soul hateth: they are a trouble unto me; I am weary to bear them. 15 And when ye spread forth your hands, I will hide mine eyes from you: yea, when ye make many prayers, I will not hear: your hands are full of blood. 16 Wash you, make you clean; put away the evil of your doings from before mine eyes; cease to do evil; 17 Learn to do well; seek judgment, relieve the oppressed, judge the fatherless, plead for the widow. 18 Come now, and let us reason together, saith the Lord: though your sins be as scarlet, they shall be as white as snow; though they be red like crimson, they shall be as wool. 19 If ye be willing and obedient, ye shall eat the good of the land: 20 But if ye refuse and rebel, ye shall be devoured with the sword: for the mouth of the Lord hath spoken it. 21 How is the faithful city become an harlot! it was full of judgment; righteousness lodged in it; but now murderers. 22 Thy silver is become dross, thy wine mixed with water: 23 Thy princes are rebellious, and companions of thieves: every one loveth gifts, and followeth after rewards: they judge not the fatherless, neither doth the cause of the widow come unto them. 24 Therefore saith the Lord, the Lord of hosts, the mighty One of Israel, Ah, I will ease me of mine adversaries, and avenge me of mine enemies: 25 And I will turn my hand upon thee, and purely purge away thy dross, and take away all thy tin: 26 And I will restore thy judges as at the first, and thy counsellors as at the beginning: afterward thou shalt be called, The city of righteousness, the faithful city. 27 Zion shall be redeemed with judgment, and her converts with righteousness. 28 And the destruction of the transgressors and of the sinners shall be together, and they that forsake the Lord shall be consumed. 29 For they shall be ashamed of the oaks which ye have desired, and ye shall be confounded for the gardens that ye have chosen. 30 For ye shall be as an oak whose leaf fadeth, and as a garden that hath no water. 31 And the strong shall be as tow, and the maker of it as a spark, and they shall both burn together, and none shall quench them.

1.2-31 This setting was the setting during the final 20 years of the reign of Uzziah. Isaiah was 20 years old when Uzziah died and Isaiah began his public ministry. National apostasy was rampant and unabated. The time for national repentance had come or judgment loomed for the nation. The sinful nation, (verse 4), had become immune to their conscience. They had lost their ability to discern right from wrong. Isaiah opens his book with the appeal to repent and the hopelessness of vain sacrifices. Israel was trying to buy off their conscience and God says it is time to forsake their wicked way. Once again the nation is given the choice to live or die. The omnipotent God calls for them to come and reason with Him. They are faced with the opportunity to change the fate of their nation.

Chapter 2

2.1 The word that Isaiah the son of Amoz saw concerning Judah and Jerusalem.

2.1 The year is 754 BC, Uzziah dies (chapter 6.1), the Northern tribe is a short 33 years from captivity (721 BC), and Isaiah pronounces the glory of Judah and Jerusalem. The next three chapters carry this theme.

2.2 And it shall come to pass in the last days, that the mountain of the Lord's house shall be established in the top of the mountains, and shall be exalted above the hills; and all nations shall flow unto it.

2.2 God's house will reign supreme over all mountains, Sinai, Carmel and Tabor. In the last days, the church Christ founds will prevail over the kingdoms of this world from sea to sea. Many people will be converted in the latter day, Zechariah 8.20-22.

2.3-7 And many people shall go and say, Come ye, and let us go up to the mountain of the Lord, to the house of the God of Jacob; and he will teach us of his ways, and we will walk in his paths: for out of Zion shall go forth the law, and the word of the Lord

from Jerusalem. 4 And he shall judge among the nations, and shall rebuke many people: and they shall beat their swords into plowshares, and their spears into pruninghooks: nation shall not lift up sword against nation, neither shall they learn war any more. 5 O house of Jacob, come ye, and let us walk in the light of the Lord. 6 Therefore thou hast forsaken thy people the house of Jacob, because they be replenished from the east, and are soothsayers like the Philistines, and they please themselves in the children of strangers. 7 Their land also is full of silver and gold, neither is there any end of their treasures; their land is also full of horses, neither is there any end of their chariots:

2.3-7 "Out of Zion. .and the word of the Lord from Jerusalem" is a prophecy of the coming of New Testament salvation recorded in Acts chapter 2. Peter preached the first sermon of the church age from Jerusalem. This new birth was the birth of the water (baptism in Jesus Name), and the birth of the spirit (outpouring of the Holy Ghost), that Jesus spoke of in John 3.1-7.

2.8-10 Their land also is full of idols; they worship the work of their own hands, that which their own fingers have made: 9 And the mean man boweth down, and the great man humbleth himself: therefore forgive them not. 10 Enter into the rock, and hide thee in the dust, for fear of the Lord, and for the glory of his majesty.

2.8-10 "Their land also is full of idols"; this is an important concept to a true child of God. We are to have no idols in our "land." This would include statues of the Virgin Mary, or statues of false gods, or departed saints, Revelation 9.20.

2.11-12 The lofty looks of man shall be humbled, and the haughtiness of men shall be bowed down, and the Lord alone shall be exalted in that day. 12 For the day of the Lord of hosts shall be upon every one that is proud and lofty, and upon every one that is lifted up; and he shall be brought low:

2.11-12 At the day of the Lord, all the followers of the antichrist shall be humbled, and the Lord alone shall be exalted, (verse 17).

2.13-22 And upon all the cedars of Lebanon, that are high and lifted up, and upon all the oaks of Bashan, 14 And upon all the high mountains, and upon all the hills that are lifted up, 15 And upon every high tower, and upon every fenced wall, 16 And upon all the ships of Tarshish, and upon all pleasant pictures. 17 And the loftiness of man shall be bowed down, and the haughtiness of men shall be made low: and the Lord alone shall be exalted in that day. 18 And the idols he shall utterly abolish. 19 And they shall go into the holes of the rocks, and into the caves of the earth, for fear of the Lord, and for the glory of his majesty, when he ariseth to shake terribly the earth. 20 In that day a man shall cast his idols of silver, and his idols of gold, which they made each one for himself to worship, to the moles and to the bats; 21 To go into the clefts of the rocks, and into the tops of the ragged rocks, for fear of the Lord, and for the glory of his majesty, when he ariseth to shake terribly the earth. 22 Cease ye from man, whose breath is in his nostrils: for wherein is he to be accounted of?

2.13-22 Oh the futility of running from God. Where would you hide that He cannot see? The irony is this: God is our hiding place. (Ps32.7) Men should run to God rather than run away and attempt to hide. Silly little gods made with human hands always fail.

Chapter 3

3.1-4 For, behold, the Lord, the Lord of hosts, doth take away from Jerusalem and from Judah the stay and the staff, the whole stay of bread, and the whole stay of water. 2 The mighty man, and the man of war, the judge, and the prophet, and the prudent, and the ancient, 3 The captain of fifty, and the honourable man, and the counsellor, and the cunning artificer, and the eloquent orator. 4 And I will give children to be their princes, and babes shall rule over them.

3.1-4 The day is coming when every man shall be equal. All titles and positions will no longer gain a man an advantage. We shall all stand before God as we came from the womb.

3.5. And the people shall be oppressed, every one by another, and every one by his neighbour: the child shall behave himself proudly against the ancient, and the base against the honourable.

3.5 "The child shall behave himself proudly against the ancient." This attitude is happening in our day. There is a loss of respect for the elders in our families and in our society.

3.6-12 When a man shall take hold of his brother of the house of his father, saying, Thou hast clothing, be thou our ruler, and let this ruin be under thy hand: 7 In that day shall he swear, saying, I will not be an healer; for in my house is neither bread nor clothing: make me not a ruler of the people. 8 For Jerusalem is ruined, and Judah is fallen: because their tongue and their doings are against the Lord, to provoke the eyes of his glory. 9 The shew of their countenance doth witness against them; and they declare their sin as Sodom, they hide it not. Woe unto their soul! for they have rewarded evil unto themselves. 10 Say ye to the righteous, that it shall be well with him: for they shall eat the fruit of their doings. 11 Woe unto the wicked! it shall be ill with him: for the reward of his hands shall be given him. 12 As for my people, children are their oppressors, and women rule over them. O my people, they which lead thee cause thee to err, and destroy the way of thy paths.

3.6-12 The chaos that comes from disaster. When the prized city of Jerusalem is fallen then mob rule and despots rise. Desperation is the mantra of the day. The sad consequence of ignoring the outstretched hand of God.

3.13-15 The Lord standeth up to plead, and standeth to judge the people. 14 The Lord will enter into judgment with the ancients of his people, and the princes thereof: for ye have eaten up the vineyard; the spoil of the poor is in your houses. 15 What mean ye that ye beat my people to pieces, and grind the faces of the poor? saith the Lord God of hosts.

3.13-15 "The Lord standeth up to plead, and standeth to

judge the people." When your Lawyer is Jesus and your Judge is Jesus, your chance of being saved is secure. There was a true void of righteous judgment so God himself steps into the "courtroom."

3.16-26 Moreover the Lord saith, Because the daughters of Zion are haughty, and walk with stretched forth necks and wanton eyes, walking and mincing as they go, and making a tinkling with their feet: 17 Therefore the Lord will smite with a scab the crown of the head of the daughters of Zion, and the Lord will discover their secret parts. 18 In that day the Lord will take away the bravery of their tinkling ornaments about their feet, and their cauls, and their round tires like the moon, 19 The chains, and the bracelets, and the mufflers, 20 The bonnets, and the ornaments of the legs, and the headbands, and the tablets, and the earrings, 21 The rings, and nose jewels, 22 The changeable suits of apparel, and the mantles, and the wimples, and the crisping pins,. 23 The glasses, and the fine linen, and the hoods, and the vails. 24 And it shall come to pass, that instead of sweet smell there shall be stink; and instead of a girdle a rent; and instead of well set hair baldness; and instead of a stomacher a girding of sackcloth; and burning instead of beauty. 25 Thy men shall fall by the sword, and thy mighty in the war. 26 And her gates shall lament and mourn; and she being desolate shall sit upon the ground.

3.16-26 In this passage God clearly lets us know his opinion of outward ornamentation. He states in strong terms it is abhorrent to Him. Although well versed in sin and old in years, the women of Jerusalem tried to maintain a youthful, childlike appearance. They therefore tripped along with short, childish steps.

God did not create the woman out of Adam's ear, lest she might become an eavesdropper, nor out of Adam's eye, lest she might become a temptress. God condemns rings, bracelets, earrings, and ornaments of the legs, nose jewels, and many other items of outward ornamentation. God wants purity in His people. This concept is continued in the New Testament when women are admonished to "adorn themselves in modest apparel…not with braided hair, or gold, or pearls," 1 Timothy 2.9.

Chapter 4

4.1 And in that day seven women shall take hold of one man, saying, We will eat our own bread, and wear our own apparel: only let us be called by thy name, to take away our reproach.

4.1 This possibly refers to the days when Pekah son of Remaliah slew in Judah 120,000 men in one day (2 Chronicles 28.6), and 200,000 women and children were also carried captive (verse 8) when war has ravaged the men, women seek for husbands among the remnant.

4.2-3 In that day shall the branch of the Lord be beautiful and glorious, and the fruit of the earth shall be excellent and comely for them that are escaped of Israel. 3 And it shall come to pass, that he that is left in Zion, and he that remaineth in Jerusalem, shall be called holy, even every one that is written among the living in Jerusalem:

4.2-3 "Branch" refers to the coming messiah, Jer 23.5, Jer 33.15, Zechariah 3.8, Zechariah 6.12, Luke 1.78.

4.4 When the Lord shall have washed away the filth of the daughters of Zion, and shall have purged the

blood of Jerusalem from the midst thereof by the spirit of judgment, and by the spirit of burning.

4.4 (Washed), Zechariah 13.1 In that day there shall be a fountain opened. for sin and uncleanness. "Spirit," whatever God does, He does by His Spirit, Psalms 104.30.

4.5 And the Lord will create upon every dwelling place of mount Zion, and upon her assemblies, a cloud and smoke by day, and the shining of a flaming fire by night: for upon all the glory shall be a defence.

4.5 God continues His acts of creation in his redeemed people. 2 Cor 4.6, Eph 2.10, Is 65.17-18

4.6 And there shall be a tabernacle for a shadow in the day time from the heat, and for a place of refuge, and for a covert from storm and from rain.

4.6 "Tabernacle," when the Glory is established in verse 5, we will see His glory manifested in the flesh (John 1.14), in John 2.21 Jesus spake of the temple of his body, and in Heb 8.2 Jesus' person is the true tabernacle which the Lord pitched and not man. Jesus is our place of refuge and our covert from the storm.

Chapter 5

5.1-2 Now will I sing to my wellbeloved a song of my beloved touching his vineyard. My wellbeloved hath a vineyard in a very fruitful hill: 2 And he fenced it, and gathered out the stones thereof, and planted it with the choicest vine, and built a tower in the midst of it, and also made a winepress therein: and he looked that it should bring forth grapes, and it brought forth wild grapes.

5.1-2 The song in this chapter is a divine echo of chapters 2 and 3. Compare 5.15-16 with 2.17, and 5.1 with 3.14 and it is obvious this song puts the former prophecies to musical score. The song continues to do this, 5.26 compared to 7.18 when the Lord hisses. Verse 25 of this chapter compared to 9.12, again shows this song encapsulates a number of prophecies. Amoz, the father of Isaiah, was brother to Amaziah king of Judah, so the King was Isaiah's uncle. John Gill commentary thinks this song was possibly written by King Amaziah. "Vineyard" is the nation of Israel, Ps 80.8, Mt 21.33. From the branch of chapter 4 verse 2, grows the vineyard of God.

5.3 And now, O inhabitants of Jerusalem, and men of Judah, judge, I pray you, betwixt me and my vineyard.

5.3 The owner of the vineyard (God) pleads with the nation to find fault with Him. Mic 6.3 states testify against me. God uses men's own mouths to condemn them when guilty, Job 15.6, Luke 19.22.

5.4 What could have been done more to my vineyard, that I have not done in it? wherefore, when I looked that it should bring forth grapes, brought it forth wild grapes?

5.4 What more could have been done for this vineyard? They were given privileges, blessings, advantages, and Divine favor. They had everything that could be desired, expected or enjoyed. After all this the harvest brought forth wild grapes.

5.5-6 And now go to; I will tell you what I will do to my vineyard: I will take away the hedge thereof, and it shall be eaten up; and break down the wall thereof, and it shall be trodden down: 6 And I will lay it waste: it shall not be pruned, nor digged; but there shall come up briers and thorns: I will also command the clouds that they rain no rain upon it.

5.5-6 This is proclaimed and fulfilled in Ps 80.12-13.

5.7 For the vineyard of the Lord of hosts is the house of Israel, and the men of Judah his pleasant plant: and he looked for judgment, but behold oppression; for righteousness, but behold a cry.

5.7 Here Isaiah proclaims the vineyard belongs to God and no other. He speaks in Amos 3.2, you only have I known of all the families of the earth. "He looked for judgment," he looked for mishpat (judgment) but found mispach (bloodshed), he looked for tsadaqua (righteousness), but found tsaaqah (cry of distress heard by God). The similarity but slight variance of these words is striking. Almost and close are not good enough for God's vineyard.

5.8 Woe unto them that join house to house, that lay field to field, till there be no place, that they may be placed alone in the midst of the earth!

5.8 Here begins the 6 "woes" of the song. The six woes are: (1) No place left for others, gathering God's blessings all to oneself (2) intemperance, wine and partying (3) persevering in sin, through the idea of laying evil eggs to hatch in the future (4) removing the distinction of right and wrong, moral perceptions removed (5) pride and arrogance (6) justifying the wicked, taking a bribe.

5.9-10 In mine ears said the Lord of hosts, Of a truth many houses shall be desolate, even great and fair, without inhabitant. 10 Yea, ten acres of vineyard shall yield one bath, and the seed of an homer shall yield an ephah.

5.9-10 "In mine ears" Is 22.14, not purged from you till ye die saith the Lord. In verse 10, the amount of land a team of oxen can plow in a whole day will yield a bath of wine. That is less than one gallon per acre. This is much like the judgment in Haggai 1.5-6, there is never enough. God is judging their greed. When they plant 65 gallons of seed it produces 5.5 gallons of harvest.

5.11-12 Woe unto them that rise up early in the morning, that they may follow strong drink; that continue until night, till wine inflame them! 12 And

the harp, and the viol, the tabret, and pipe, and wine, are in their feasts: but they regard not the work of the Lord, neither consider the operation of his hands.**

5.11-12 The second woe, intemperance, drinking and partying (verse12), with no time for God. Interesting that the tabret is mentioned, this is the instrument used in drowning out the cries of the children sacrificed to Moloch; for which Tophet is named. Music was common at ancient feasts, Is 24.8, Amos 6.5-6.

5.13 Therefore my people are gone into captivity, because they have no knowledge: and their honourable men are famished, and their multitude dried up with thirst.

5.13 "Knowledge" A lack of knowledge and rejection of knowledge brings destruction on the people, and judgment on their children, Hosea 4.6, Luke 19.44. 2 Kings 17.6 is the fulfillment of the captivity that would come.

5.14 Therefore hell hath enlarged herself, and opened her mouth without measure: and their glory, and their multitude, and their pomp, and he that rejoiceth, shall descend into it.

5.14 "Hell" here would be sheol, or the grave, indicating the famine would be so great many would die.

5.15-16 And the mean man shall be brought down, and the mighty man shall be humbled, and the eyes of the lofty shall be humbled: 16 But the Lord of hosts shall be exalted in judgment, and God that is holy shall be sanctified in righteousness.

5.15-16 The mean and mighty men will be brought down and the Lord will be exalted

5.17 Then shall the lambs feed after their manner, and the waste places of the fat ones shall strangers eat.

5.17 Is a promise of restoration of God's flock Micah 2.12, when God gathers all of Israel as His sheep.

5.18-19 Woe unto them that draw iniquity with cords of vanity, and sin as it were with a cart rope: 19 That say, Let him make speed, and hasten his work, that we may see it: and let the counsel of the Holy One of Israel draw nigh and come, that we may know it!

5.18-19 Begins the third woe. These workers of sin challenge God. Jer 17.15 Where is the word of the Lord? 2 Peter 3.3-4 there shall come scoffers in the last days. These evil men laugh at God and mock His word, and in verse 19 actually challenge God.

5.20 Woe unto them that call evil good, and good evil; that put darkness for light, and light for darkness; that put bitter for sweet, and sweet for bitter!

5.20 Begins the fourth woe. This is the evil men who remove the distinctions between right and wrong. This would be the case with many of the Scribes and Pharisees of Jesus' day.

5.21 Woe unto them that are wise in their own eyes, and prudent in their own sight!

5.21 Begins the fifth woe. This is pride and arrogance. Is 29.14-15 tells us this "wisdom" will perish.

5.22-23 Woe unto them that are mighty to drink wine, and men of strength to mingle strong drink: 23 Which justify the wicked for reward, and take away the righteousness of the righteous from him!

5.22-23 Thus begins the sixth and final woe of the song. These are corrupt judges who are given to wine and wrong. They take bribes, such as the indulgences of the Catholic church during the reformation. They justify the wicked for reward.

5.24-30 Therefore as the fire devoureth the stubble, and the flame consumeth the chaff, so their root shall be as rottenness, and their blossom shall go up as dust: because they have cast away the law of the Lord of hosts, and despised the word of the Holy One of Israel. 25 Therefore is the anger of the Lord kindled against his people, and he hath stretched forth his hand against them, and hath smitten them: and the hills did tremble, and their carcases were torn in the midst of the streets. For all this his anger is not turned away, but his hand is stretched out still. 26 And he will lift up an ensign to the nations from far, and will hiss unto them from the end of the earth: and, behold, they shall come with speed swiftly: 27 None shall be weary nor stumble among them; none shall slumber nor sleep; neither shall the girdle of their loins be loosed, nor the latchet of their shoes be broken: 28 Whose arrows are sharp, and all their bows bent, their horses' hoofs shall be counted like flint, and their wheels like a whirlwind: 29 Their roaring shall be like a lion, they shall roar like young lions: yea, they shall roar, and lay hold of the prey, and shall carry it away safe, and none shall deliver it. 30 And in that day they shall roar against them like the roaring of the

sea: and if one look unto the land, behold darkness and sorrow, and the light is darkened in the heavens thereof.

5.24-30 The song concludes with God producing judgmental fire to burn up the chaff from the wheat, much the same as is mentioned in the New Testament, Mt 3.12. When the fire of judgment once begins it will continue to burn. For all this His anger is not turned away, (verse 25). Thus ends the first song of Isaiah written in the reign of King Jotham.

Chapter 6

6.1 In the year that king Uzziah died I saw also the Lord sitting upon a throne, high and lifted up, and his train filled the temple.

6.1 This a pivotal moment in the life of the young prophet. It seems this is the first and only time he has a vision, although other prophets have visions frequently. The "Lord" Isaiah saw was Jesus according to John 12.41.

6.2-3 Above it stood the seraphims: each one had six wings; with twain he covered his face, and with twain he covered his feet, and with twain he did fly. 3 And one cried unto another, and said, Holy, holy, holy, is the Lord of hosts: the whole earth is full of his glory.

6.2-3 Seraphim: seraph is to burn. This reflects burning zeal and dazzling brightness, these beings have 6 wings and human hands and voice. They cry holy, holy, holy. See Rev 4.8.

6.4 And the posts of the door moved at the voice of him that cried, and the house was filled with smoke.

6.4 Smoke: the Shekinah cloud, 1 K 8.10, Ez 10.4. This

may also refer to the earthquake during Uzziah's reign Zec 14.5.

6.5 Then said I, Woe is me! for I am undone; because I am a man of unclean lips, and I dwell in the midst of a people of unclean lips: for mine eyes have seen the King, the Lord of hosts.

6.5 I am undone is a common reaction when in God's presence, Jud 6.22, Jud 13.22, Job 42.5, Luke 5.8, Rev 1.17.

6.6-7 Then flew one of the seraphims unto me, having a live coal in his hand, which he had taken with the tongs from off the altar: 7 And he laid it upon my mouth, and said, Lo, this hath touched thy lips; and thine iniquity is taken away, and thy sin purged.

6.6-7 The coal placed upon the lips and iniquity and sin being purged foreshadowed the coming Day of Pentecost in Acts 2, when cloven tongues of fire came accompanied by a rushing mighty wind. Mal 3.2 the refiners fire. The prophet's mouth was his method to reach the people, therefore it is cleansed.

6.8 Also I heard the voice of the Lord, saying, Whom shall I send, and who will go for us? Then said I, Here am I; send me.

6.8 After the cleansing came the call. Personal experience must precede public service. Isaiah accepts his call at the approximate age of 20 years old.

6.9 And he said, Go, and tell this people, Hear ye

indeed, but understand not; and see ye indeed, but perceive not.

6.9 God sends people to offer deliverance even when His omniscience knows they will not accept, so that none may be without excuse, Rom 1.20.

6.10 Make the heart of this people fat, and make their ears heavy, and shut their eyes; lest they see with their eyes, and hear with their ears, and understand with their heart, and convert, and be healed.

6.10 The long suffering of God was drawing to a close with the nation. Jesus spoke of this tendency in Mt 13.14. Their deafness refrained them from being healed, Is 1.6

6.11 Then said I, Lord, how long? And he answered, Until the cities be wasted without inhabitant, and the houses without man, and the land be utterly desolate,

6.11 The Babylonian invasion is foretold here.

6.12 And the Lord have removed men far away, and there be a great forsaking in the midst of the land.

6.12 Jer 4.29

6.13 But yet in it shall be a tenth, and it shall return, and shall be eaten: as a teil tree, and as an oak, whose substance is in them, when they cast their leaves: so the holy seed shall be the substance thereof.

6.13 "The holy seed," this foretells the remnant of the nation returning from Babylon and also the fulfilling of Israel's promises in the New Testament, Rom 11.5.

Chapter 7

7.1 And it came to pass in the days of Ahaz the son of Jotham, the son of Uzziah, king of Judah, that Rezin the king of Syria, and Pekah the son of Remaliah, king of Israel, went up toward Jerusalem to war against it, but could not prevail against it.

7.1 2 Ch 28.5 is Ahaz great defeat. These Kings were trying to force Judah to form an alliance against Tiglath-pilesar of Assyria. Ahaz initially loses in a great slaughter.

7.2 And it was told the house of David, saying, Syria is confederate with Ephraim. And his heart was moved, and the heart of his people, as the trees of the wood are moved with the wind.

7.2 Ephraim is the 10 Northern tribes.

7.3 Then said the Lord unto Isaiah, Go forth now to meet Ahaz, thou, and Shearjashub thy son, at the end of the conduit of the upper pool in the highway of the fuller's field;

7.3 Shearjashub means a remnant shall return

7.4-5 And say unto him, Take heed, and be quiet; fear not, neither be fainthearted for the two tails of these smoking firebrands, for the fierce anger of Rezin with Syria, and of the son of Remaliah. 5 Because Syria, Ephraim, and the son of Remaliah, have taken evil counsel against thee, saying,

7.4-5 Son of Remaliah is Pekah 2 K 15.25

7.6 Let us go up against Judah, and vex it, and let us make a breach therein for us, and set a king in the midst of it, even the son of Tabeal:

7.6 Their goal was to divide Judah among themselves

7.7 Thus saith the Lord God, It shall not stand, neither shall it come to pass.

7.7 Is 8.10, Pr 21.30

7.8 For the head of Syria is Damascus, and the head of Damascus is Rezin; and within threescore and five years shall Ephraim be broken, that it be not a people

7.8 One deportation happened in one to two years (2K 15.29), another after 20 years (2K 17.1-6), The final one after 65 years (2K 17.24; 2Ch 33.11).

7.9-10 And the head of Ephraim is Samaria, and the head of Samaria is Remaliah's son. If ye will not believe, surely ye shall not be established. 10 Moreover the Lord spake again unto Ahaz, saying,

7.9-10 This is a paronomasia in the Hebrew. If ye will

not confide ye shall not abide. If ye will not be faithful ye will not be established.

7.11 Ask thee a sign of the Lord thy God; ask it either in the depth, or in the height above.

7.11 Ask. Since you don't believe Isaiah, let me prove it to you. Sign= a miracle. Ask big or deep.

7.12 But Ahaz said, I will not ask, neither will I tempt the Lord.

7.12 There are several reasons Ahaz may have refused. He may not have wanted to tempt God. He may have thought the local God of Syria was more powerful, or he may not have wanted to identify with God over Syria.

7.13 And he said, Hear ye now, O house of David; Is it a small thing for you to weary men, but will ye weary my God also?

7.13 Isaiah alludes to David in contrast to his degenerate descendant Ahaz.

7.14 Therefore the Lord himself shall give you a sign; Behold, a virgin shall conceive, and bear a son, and shall call his name Immanuel.

7.14 Since Ahaz rejects the offer of a sign, God designs to give him one. Virgin is a word meaning "to lie hid." The article here infers a particular virgin, which is in reference to Mt 1.23. We know this because her child is to be called Immanuel (God with us). Further we know this because Is 9.6 also speaks of Christ. 1 Ti 3.16, Col 2.9

7.15-16 Butter and honey shall he eat, that he may know to refuse the evil, and choose the good. 16 For before the child shall know to refuse the evil, and choose the good, the land that thou abhorrest shall be forsaken of both her kings.

7.15-16 Reverts back to the primary interpretation, and predicts in two years Syria and Ephraim will be forsaken. At about three years of age moral consciousness begins.

7.17-25 The Lord shall bring upon thee, and upon thy people, and upon thy father's house, days that have not come, from the day that Ephraim departed from Judah; even the king of Assyria. 18 And it shall come to pass in that day, that the Lord shall hiss for the fly that is in the uttermost part of the rivers of Egypt, and for the bee that is in the land of Assyria. 19 And they shall come, and shall rest all of them in the desolate valleys, and in the holes of the rocks, and upon all thorns, and upon all bushes. 20 In the same day shall the Lord shave with a razor that is hired, namely, by them beyond the river, by the king of Assyria, the head, and the hair of the feet: and it shall also consume the beard. 21 And it shall come to pass in that day, that a man shall nourish a young cow, and two sheep; 22 And it shall come to pass, for the abundance of milk that they shall give he shall eat butter: for butter and honey shall every one eat that is left in the land. 23 And it shall come to pass in that day, that every place shall be, where there were a thousand vines at a thousand silverlings, it shall even be for briers and thorns. 24 With arrows and with bows shall men come thither; because all the land shall become briers and thorns. 25 And on all hills that shall be digged with the mattock, there shall not come thither the fear of

briers and thorns: but it shall be for the sending forth of oxen, and for the treading of lesser cattle.

7.17-25 Temporary deliverance was given, but final deliverance would eventually come through Messiah.

7.18 The fly represents Egypt and the bee represents Assyria. Within 2 years of Isaiah's prophecy, Syria fell to Assyria. Pekah no longer ruled Israel and within 10 years Israel also fell to Assyria.

7.20 To shave the beard and body was a great indignity to an easterner.

7.21-23 The crops will have vanished and the land will have become a pasture.

7.24 The land will become a place of wild beasts

7.25 Fulfilling Is 5.6

Chapter 8

8.1-5 Moreover the Lord said unto me, Take thee a great roll, and write in it with a man's pen concerning Mahershalalhashbaz. 2 And I took unto me faithful witnesses to record, Uriah the priest, and Zechariah the son of Jeberechiah. 3 And I went unto the prophetess; and she conceived, and bare a son. Then said the Lord to me, Call his name Mahershalalhashbaz. 4 For before the child shall have knowledge to cry, My father, and my mother, the riches of Damascus and the spoil of Samaria shall be taken away before the king of Assyria. 5 The Lord spake also unto me again, saying,

8.1-4 Chapter eight is a continuation of the previous chapter in announcing the coming events of judgment. Isaiah is commanded to take a great roll and write the name of his son on it Maher-shalal-hash-baz (speed the spoil or hasten the prey). This notified the nation that swift Assyrian judgment was on its way. A great roll able to be read by all, in simple language so afterward all would know God prophesied this and Isaiah predicted it.

8.2 Uriah as a witness would prove the accuracy, as he was an accomplice to Ahaz. 2K 16.10

8.4-5 Before the child is three, these events will transpire. This prophecy is at a later time for the time is shortened, and verses 17, 21-22 also indicate more calamity.

8.6-7 Forasmuch as this people refuseth the waters of Shiloah that go softly, and rejoice in Rezin and Remaliah's son; 7 Now therefore, behold, the Lord bringeth up upon them the waters of the river, strong and many, even the king of Assyria, and all his glory: and he shall come up over all his channels, and go over all his banks:

8.6-7 The waters of Siloam refer to the impending judgment that will ultimately heal the nation, as the pool of Siloam was known for healing properties. These waters will flow over Judah and Immanuel will bring healing afterwards. The waters will reach the neck but the head (Jerusalem) will not drown.

8.8-10 And he shall pass through Judah; he shall overflow and go over, he shall reach even to the neck; and the stretching out of his wings shall fill the breadth of thy land, O Immanuel. 9 Associate yourselves, O ye people, and ye shall be broken in pieces; and give ear, all ye of far countries: gird yourselves, and ye shall be broken in pieces; gird yourselves, and ye shall be broken in pieces. 10 Take counsel together, and it shall come to nought; speak the word, and it shall not stand: for God is with us.

8.8-10 Immanuel (God is with us) is the true owner of this land.

8.11-18 For the Lord spake thus to me with a strong hand, and instructed me that I should not walk in

the way of this people, saying, 12 Say ye not, A confederacy, to all them to whom this people shall say, A confederacy; neither fear ye their fear, nor be afraid. 13 Sanctify the Lord of hosts himself; and let him be your fear, and let him be your dread. 14 And he shall be for a sanctuary; but for a stone of stumbling and for a rock of offence to both the houses of Israel, for a gin and for a snare to the inhabitants of Jerusalem. 15 And many among them shall stumble, and fall, and be broken, and be snared, and be taken. 16 Bind up the testimony, seal the law among my disciples. 17 And I will wait upon the Lord, that hideth his face from the house of Jacob, and I will look for him. 18 Behold, I and the children whom the Lord hath given me are for signs and for wonders in Israel from the Lord of hosts, which dwelleth in mount Zion.

8.11-18 Stone of stumbling. . Rock of offence, is quoted in Rom 9.33 and 1 Pet 2.8, this is Jesus Christ. Gin= trap, some find refuge in Jesus, others are trapped in unbelief. The immediate fulfillment was for those who rejected Isaiah's prophecy of coming judgment.

8.13 Sanctify, Is 29.23, Nu 20.12

8.14 The prophecy extends to both the house of Israel and the House of Judah, therefore it extends beyond the time of Ahaz.

8.17 Whatever the rest of the nation does, I will wait upon the Lord Hab 2.3

8.18 This is quoted in Heb 2.13 proving again this is for future fulfillment. The wonder is messiah will be father and son. Is 9.6. We are His children (Heb 2.13), yet also His brothers and His friends.

8.19-22 And when they shall say unto you, Seek unto them that have familiar spirits, and unto wizards that peep, and that mutter: should not a people seek unto their God? for the living to the dead? 20 To the law and to the testimony: if they speak not according to this word, it is because there is no light in them. 21 And they shall pass through it, hardly bestead and hungry: and it shall come to pass, that when they shall be hungry, they shall fret themselves, and curse their king and their God, and look upward. 22 And they shall look unto the earth; and behold trouble and darkness, dimness of anguish; and they shall be driven to darkness.

8.19-22 The people are warned to not seek wizards or any form of witchcraft in their desperation.

Chapter 9

9.1-5 Nevertheless the dimness shall not be such as was in her vexation, when at the first he lightly afflicted the land of Zebulun and the land of Naphtali, and afterward did more grievously afflict her by the way of the sea, beyond Jordan, in Galilee of the nations. 2 The people that walked in darkness have seen a great light: they that dwell in the land of the shadow of death, upon them hath the light shined. 3 Thou hast multiplied the nation, and not increased the joy: they joy before thee according to the joy in harvest, and as men rejoice when they divide the spoil. 4 For thou hast broken the yoke of his burden, and the staff of his shoulder, the rod of his oppressor, as in the day of Midian. 5 For every battle of the warrior is with confused noise, and garments rolled in blood; but this shall be with burning and fuel of fire.

9.1-5 The northern tribes would be affected first by the invasion of Assyria, so they are assured of dimness. This region had already felt the Assyrian captivity 2K 15.29. This area was the first to receive the Assyrian invasion and also the first to receive the joyous news of Messiah Mt 4.13-16, Ps 68.27-28.

9.6-7 For unto us a child is born, unto us a son is given: and the government shall be upon his shoulder: and his name shall be called Wonderful, Counsellor, The mighty God, The everlasting Father, The Prince of Peace. 7 Of the increase of his government and peace there shall be no end, upon the throne of David, and upon his kingdom, to order it, and to establish it with judgment and with justice from henceforth even for ever. The zeal of the Lord of hosts will perform this.

9.6-7 This is prophetic of Jesus Christ, the coming messiah. No other child has ever been or will ever be all of these things. Jesus Christ is wonderful, counselor, the mighty God, the everlasting father, and the prince of peace. This is fulfilled in the New Testament, 1 Tim 3.16. Col 2.8-10, Jn 14.9, Jn 10.30. The son in this prophecy is called the Everlasting Father (abiad), which means the father of eternity. The prophesied Immanuel now takes definite clarity; He is God incarnate, Jesus Christ of the New Testament.

9.7 Messiah's rule will have no end Da 2.44. It will be a kingdom of justice and judgment.

9.8-10.4 *This section of Isaiah's prophecy continues until 10.4. These chapters were divided by Cardinal Hugo in AD1250, and into verses by Robert Stephens in AD1551.*

9.8-12 The Lord sent a word into Jacob, and it hath lighted upon Israel. 9 And all the people shall know, even Ephraim and the inhabitant of Samaria, that say in the pride and stoutness of heart, 10 The bricks are fallen down, but we will build with hewn stones: the sycomores are cut down, but we will change them into cedars. 11 Therefore the Lord shall set up

the adversaries of Rezin against him, and join his enemies together; 12 The Syrians before, and the Philistines behind; and they shall devour Israel with open mouth. For all this his anger is not turned away, but his hand is stretched out still.

9.8-12 The destruction of Northern Israel by the Assyrian army will not be rebuilt. This possibly refers to the 10 tribes being carried away and never returning in mass. Israel was invaded by Tiglath-Pileser in 732BC. In a little over 10 years he would come again and march to the very gates of Jerusalem.

9.13 For the people turneth not unto him that smiteth them, neither do they seek the Lord of hosts.

9.13 The people still remain obstinate in heart.

9.14 Therefore the Lord will cut off from Israel head and tail, branch and rush, in one day.

9.14 The nation will lose its place of prominence De 28.13

9.15-21 The ancient and honourable, he is the head; and the prophet that teacheth lies, he is the tail. 16 For the leaders of this people cause them to err; and they that are led of them are destroyed. 17 Therefore the Lord shall have no joy in their young men, neither shall have mercy on their fatherless and widows: for every one is an hypocrite and an evildoer, and every mouth speaketh folly. For all this his anger is not turned away, but his hand is stretched out still. 18 For wickedness burneth as the fire: it shall devour the briers and thorns, and shall kindle in the thickets of

the forest, and they shall mount up like the lifting up of smoke. 19 Through the wrath of the Lord of hosts is the land darkened, and the people shall be as the fuel of the fire: no man shall spare his brother. 20 And he shall snatch on the right hand, and be hungry; and he shall eat on the left hand, and they shall not be satisfied: they shall eat every man the flesh of his own arm: 21 Manasseh, Ephraim; and Ephraim, Manasseh: and they together shall be against Judah. For all this his anger is not turned away, but his hand is stretched out still.

9.15-21 The people show no inclination to repent or turn from their sinful ways, so judgment is imminent. Finally in verse 21 even Manasseh and Ephraim turn upon one another thirsting for one another's blood, and the final defeat comes.

Chapter 10

10.1-4 Woe unto them that decree unrighteous decrees, and that write grievousness which they have prescribed; 2 To turn aside the needy from judgment, and to take away the right from the poor of my people, that widows may be their prey, and that they may rob the fatherless! 3 And what will ye do in the day of visitation, and in the desolation which shall come from far? to whom will ye flee for help? and where will ye leave your glory? 4 Without me they shall bow down under the prisoners, and they shall fall under the slain. For all this his anger is not turned away, but his hand is stretched out still.

10.1-4 These verses are connected to the prophecy in chapter 9.

10.1 Them that decree. .the magistrates who caused unjust decisions.

10.3 There will be no escape in that day

10.5-32 *Is a hymn of praise about the destruction of the Assyrians and the coming of the messiah. Is10.9, 11 show that Samaria was destroyed before this song. This prophecy is one of the first under Hezekiah, probably between 722 and 715 BC.*

10.5-6 O Assyrian, the rod of mine anger, and the staff in their hand is mine indignation. 6 I will send him against an hypocritical nation, and against the people of my wrath will I give him a charge, to take the spoil, and to take the prey, and to tread them down like the mire of the streets.

10.5-6 God uses Assyria as his rod to correct His people, in verse 6 this rod is used against a hypocritical nation.

10.7 Howbeit he meaneth not so, neither doth his heart think so; but it is in his heart to destroy and cut off nations not a few.

10.7 God uses the unknowing to accomplish His will and intent, while they believe it is all their idea.

10.8 For he saith, Are not my princes altogether kings?

10.8 Eastern satraps and governors often had the title of king. This is another reason Jesus is always the "King of kings"

10.9-11 Is not Calno as Carchemish? is not Hamath as Arpad? is not Samaria as Damascus? 10 As my hand hath found the kingdoms of the idols, and whose graven images did excel them of Jerusalem and of Samaria; 11 Shall I not, as I have done unto Samaria and her idols, so do to Jerusalem and her idols?

10.9-11 Rabshekah's boast, verse 10-11 is a double protasis to the hymn.

10.12 Wherefore it shall come to pass, that when the Lord hath performed his whole work upon mount Zion and on Jerusalem, I will punish the fruit of the stout heart of the king of Assyria, and the glory of his high looks.

10.12 The events happening here are but a part of God's grander plan. When God is finished with Jerusalem, He will deal with Assyria.

10.13-15 For he saith, By the strength of my hand I have done it, and by my wisdom; for I am prudent: and I have removed the bounds of the people, and have robbed their treasures, and I have put down the inhabitants like a valiant man: 14 And my hand hath found as a nest the riches of the people: and as one gathereth eggs that are left, have I gathered all the earth; and there was none that moved the wing, or opened the mouth, or peeped. 15 Shall the axe boast itself against him that heweth therewith? or shall the saw magnify itself against him that shaketh it? as if the rod should shake itself against them that lift it up, or as if the staff should lift up itself, as if it were no wood.

10.13-15 Here The Assyrian leader makes the mistake of many in that he thinks it is his acumen that has brought this success. He is unaware of the hand of the Almighty on his life. Verse 15 has Isaiah clarifying who really controls destinies. The Assyrian is merely a tool in the hand of the King of kings.

10.16-23 Therefore shall the Lord, the Lord of hosts, send among his fat ones leanness; and under his glory he shall kindle a burning like the burning of a fire. 17

And the light of Israel shall be for a fire, and his Holy One for a flame: and it shall burn and devour his thorns and his briers in one day; 18 And shall consume the glory of his forest, and of his fruitful field, both soul and body: and they shall be as when a standard-bearer fainteth. 19 And the rest of the trees of his forest shall be few, that a child may write them. 20 And it shall come to pass in that day, that the remnant of Israel, and such as are escaped of the house of Jacob, shall no more again stay upon him that smote them; but shall stay upon the Lord, the Holy One of Israel, in truth. 21 The remnant shall return, even the remnant of Jacob, unto the mighty God. 22 For though thy people Israel be as the sand of the sea, yet a remnant of them shall return: the consumption decreed shall overflow with righteousness. 23 For the Lord God of hosts shall make a consumption, even determined, in the midst of all the land.

10.16-23 When the Lord is finished with the Rod of Assyria, the remnant of the people of God shall return. Verse 23 speaks the end is already determined, and this leads to the crescendo of the hymn, this Assyrian trouble is but for a time, then God's people will again triumph.

10.19-21 The destruction shall be so vast, a child can count the remains

10.22 Quoted by Paul in Rom 9.27

10.24-34 *God assures His people He has everything in control and this tempest will pass. One of the great themes of Isaiah we see repeated many times is the triumph of God's eternal purpose (Eph 3.11). God will triumph. Acts 15.18*

10.24-26 Therefore thus saith the Lord God of hosts, O my people that dwellest in Zion, be not afraid of the Assyrian: he shall smite thee with a rod, and shall lift up his staff against thee, after the manner of Egypt. 25 For yet a very little while, and the indignation shall cease, and mine anger in their destruction. 26 And the Lord of hosts shall stir up a scourge for him according to the slaughter of Midian at the rock of Oreb: and as his rod was upon the sea, so shall he lift it up after the manner of Egypt.

10.24-26 Even in their hypocrisy, God still owns them. .Oh my people

10.27 And it shall come to pass in that day, that his burden shall be taken away from off thy shoulder, and his yoke from off thy neck, and the yoke shall be destroyed because of the anointing.

10.27 Judah was still a tributary to Assyria. Hezekiah would revolt at the beginning of Sennacherib's reign.

10.28-32 He is come to Aiath, he is passed to Migron; at Michmash he hath laid up his carriages: 29 They are gone over the passage: they have taken up their lodging at Geba; Ramah is afraid; Gibeah of Saul is fled. 30 Lift up thy voice, O daughter of Gallim: cause it to be heard unto Laish, O poor Anathoth. 31 Madmenah is removed; the inhabitants of Gebim gather themselves to flee. 32 As yet shall he remain at Nob that day: he shall shake his hand against the mount of the daughter of Zion, the hill of Jerusalem.

10.28-32 Documents the advance of the Assyrian army

10.33-34 Behold, the Lord, the Lord of hosts, shall lop the bough with terror: and the high ones of stature shall be hewn down, and the haughty shall be humbled. 34 And he shall cut down the thickets of the forest with iron, and Lebanon shall fall by a mighty one.

10.33-34 The ax that fell the forest shall feel the same blade of judgment. 2K 19.35, 185,000 Assyrians fall in one night when Sennacherib is overthrown by the angel of God. Vengeance ultimately belongs to God.

Chapter 11

11.1 And there shall come forth a rod out of the stem of Jesse, and a Branch shall grow out of his roots:

11.1 This chapter is vintage Isaiah. It is eloquent and majestic in foretelling the branch and the root of Jesse. The prophecy is about the coming of Jesus Christ to the world. Jesus will grow out of Jesse's stem and then become the branch that fills the earth, eventually providing a highway to heaven. The overview and big picture of this chapter is enormous. It foretells the coming millennial reign of Jesus Christ, when Christ will ascend His rightful throne as "King of kings"

11.1 Jer 23.5, 33.15 also foretell the Branch as being Jesus Christ. The Hebrew word for branch used here is "neser," not the more common word "semach" which is used in Jeremiah. The word neser is the root of "Nazareth." Because Nazareth is not mentioned in the Old Testament this is relevant to further pinpointing Jesus as the coming Messiah. Rom 15.12

11.2-5 And the spirit of the Lord shall rest upon him, the spirit of wisdom and understanding, the spirit of counsel and might, the spirit of knowledge and of

the fear of the Lord; 3 And shall make him of quick understanding in the fear of the Lord: and he shall not judge after the sight of his eyes, neither reprove after the hearing of his ears: 4 But with righteousness shall he judge the poor, and reprove with equity for the meek of the earth: and he shall smite the earth: with the rod of his mouth, and with the breath of his lips shall he slay the wicked. 5 And righteousness shall be the girdle of his loins, and faithfulness the girdle of his reins.

11.2-5 The Old Testament people were familiar with the Spirit of the Lord coming upon people for the last 650 years dating back to the Judges. Is 61.1 and Luke 4.18 speak that Jesus claimed this anointing for himself. The spirit of counsel and might are the same words used in Is 9.6 to the child born messiah.

11.6-9 The wolf also shall dwell with the lamb, and the leopard shall lie down with the kid; and the calf and the young lion and the fatling together; and a little child shall lead them. 7 And the cow and the bear shall feed; their young ones shall lie down together: and the lion shall eat straw like the ox. 8 And the sucking child shall play on the hole of the asp, and the weaned child shall put his hand on the cockatrice' den. 9 They shall not hurt nor destroy in all my holy mountain: for the earth shall be full of the knowledge of the Lord, as the waters cover the sea.

11.6-9 The millennial reign of Jesus Christ is here described. The painting by Edward Hicks, Peaceable Kingdom is noted for this. It portrays violent animals succumbing to the all-powerful nature of Christ that overcomes their natural tendency to destroy. Each animal is paired with its natural prey. When Christ sits on His throne his power will be such that even the animal kingdom is dominated and subdued. Nothing shall hurt or destroy in all His Holy mountain. A lion eats straw, venomous creatures will not harm a child, and the earth will be full of the knowledge of the Lord. Christ will reign over a perfect government for 1000 years, Rev 20.2. This reign before the final White Throne Judgment will prove to the world that God is just in his final judgment. Man will live in a perfect environment and when Satan is loosed after 1000 years man's heart is proven again to be rooted in sin and rebellion, and man revolts against God's perfect and peaceable government. The heart of man is intrinsically evil and can only be changed and controlled by the indwelling spirit of God. To have this indwelling power to overcome, man must be born again of the water and spirit spoken of in Jn 3.1-7.

11.10-16 And in that day there shall be a root of Jesse, which shall stand for an ensign of the people; to it shall the Gentiles seek: and his rest shall be glorious. 11 And it shall come to pass in that day, that the Lord shall set his hand again the second time to recover the remnant of his people, which shall be left, from Assyria, and from Egypt, and from Pathros, and from Cush, and from Elam, and from Shinar, and from Hamath, and from the islands of the sea. 12 And he shall set up an ensign for the nations, and shall assemble the outcasts of Israel, and gather together the dispersed of Judah from the four corners of the earth. 13 The envy also of Ephraim shall depart, and the adversaries of Judah shall be cut off: Ephraim shall not envy Judah, and Judah shall not vex Ephraim. 14 But they shall fly upon the shoulders of the Philistines toward the

west; they shall spoil them of the east together: they shall lay their hand upon Edom and Moab; and the children of Ammon shall obey them. 15 And the Lord shall utterly destroy the tongue of the Egyptian sea; and with his mighty wind shall he shake his hand over the river, and shall smite it in the seven streams, and make men go over dryshod. 16 And there shall be an highway for the remnant of his people, which shall be left, from Assyria; like as it was to Israel in the day that he came up out of the land of Egypt.

11.10 Gentiles will also be included in Christ's kingdom; this has been part of the eternal purpose of God before the world began. Eph 3.9-11. Jesus was the "shoot from the root," Is 53.2, Rev 22.16

11.10-16 The millennial reign of peace extends further than the animal kingdom, it also envelops the enemies of Israel. Peace shall reign supreme when the Prince of peace ascends His earthly throne. Is 9.6. Christ will be the "ensign" for all nations. He will be King over all the earth that He created Col 1.16

Chapter 12

12.1-6 And in that day thou shalt say, O Lord, I will praise thee: though thou wast angry with me, thine anger is turned away, and thou comfortedst me. 2 Behold, God is my salvation; I will trust, and not be afraid: for the Lord Jehovah is my strength and my song; he also is become my salvation. 3 Therefore with joy shall ye draw water out of the wells of salvation. 4 And in that day shall ye say, Praise the Lord, call upon his name, declare his doings among the people, make mention that his name is exalted. . . 5 Sing unto the Lord; for he hath done excellent things: this is known in all the earth. . 6 Cry out and shout, thou inhabitant of Zion: for great is the Holy One of Israel in the midst of thee.

12.1-6 The first section of Isaiah's prophecy comes to a close with this captivating song of praise and glory to Jehovah the savior. Isaiah borrows a line from Miriam's song of deliverance (Ex 15.12), at the end of verse 2. God has, and will again, deliver His people. The mastery and imagery of Isaiah is seen in this passage and is one of the windows to look in and see why Isaiah is. referred to as the Shakespeare of Hebrew literature.

12.2 Strength. .song. .salvation, derived from Ex 15.12, Ps 118.14, the idea of salvation was associated with the Feast of Tabernacles, hence when Jesus enters Jerusalem in Mt 21.9 the cry of the masses was Hosanna, meaning "save we beseech thee."

12.3 Water. .an expressive image in a hot country. On the last day of the feast of tabernacles it was the custom of the Jews to bring water in a golden pot from the fountain of Siloam and pour it mixed with wine on the sacrifice on the altar. This is the allusion in Jesus' words in Jn 7.2, 37-39 where the pouring out of the water signifies the future outpouring of the Spirit of God on the day of Pentecost in Acts 2.1-4. This flow will be from wells that are ever producing, not streams that can run dry in certain seasons. These living waters are spoken of in Jn 4.14 and Rev 7.17.

12.6 the doxology of chapters 1-12 thus ends with the declaration "great is the Holy One of Israel in the midst of thee." God has not left them nor forsaken them, He is ever their God; therefore they are to sing exuberantly.

Chapters 13-23 contain prophecies to foreign nations. This is one element that puts Isaiah in the Major prophet status, the breath of his writing have far reaching fulfillment.

13.1 The burden of Babylon, which Isaiah the son of Amoz did see.

13.1 The burden (masa') of Isaiah can also be rendered oracle. Isaiah saw this prophecy. There is a certain comfort in knowing God is fair in his judgment. The previous section dealt with his righteous judgment upon His rebellious children, the nation of Israel. Now we see God is fair in turning the same measure of righteous judgment upon the nations who surround Israel. This prevents the chosen nation from despair, or turning to human confederacies. These prophecies are given in the right chronological place concerning Western Asia.

13.2-5 Lift ye up a banner upon the high mountain, exalt the voice unto them, shake the hand, that they may go into the gates of the nobles. 3 I have commanded my sanctified ones, I have also called my mighty ones for mine anger, even them that rejoice in my highness. 4 The noise of a multitude in the mountains, like as of a great people; a tumultuous noise of the kingdoms of nations gathered together: the Lord of hosts mustereth the host of the battle. 5 They come from a far country, from the end of heaven, even the Lord, and the weapons of his indignation, to destroy the whole land.

13.2-5 The people are assured the same terrible dirge will fall upon the very ones who propagated it upon Israel. This retribution would one day encourage the remnant on the banks of Chebar Ps 137.9 Enemies will one day rape the women of Babylon just like the fate that befell the women of Judah. Lam 5.11.

13.6-18 6 Howl ye; for the day of the Lord is at hand; it shall come as a destruction from the Almighty. 7 Therefore shall all hands be faint, and every man's heart shall melt: 8 And they shall be afraid: pangs and sorrows shall take hold of them; they shall be in pain as a woman that travaileth: they shall be amazed one at another; their faces shall be as flames.

9 Behold, the day of the Lord cometh, cruel both with wrath and fierce anger, to lay the land desolate: and he shall destroy the sinners thereof out of it. 10 For the stars of heaven and the constellations thereof shall not give their light: the sun shall be darkened in his going forth, and the moon shall not cause her light to shine. 11 And I will punish the world for their evil, and the wicked for their iniquity; and I will cause the arrogancy of the proud to cease, and will lay low the haughtiness of the terrible. 12 I will make a man more precious than fine gold; even a man than the golden wedge of Ophir. 13 Therefore I will shake the heavens, and the earth shall remove out of her place, in the wrath of the Lord of hosts, and in the day of his fierce anger. 14 And it shall be as the chased roe, and as a sheep that no man taketh up: they shall every man turn to his own people, and flee every one into his own land. 15 Every one that is found shall be thrust through; and every one that is joined unto them shall fall by the sword. 16 Their children also shall be dashed to pieces before their eyes; their houses shall be spoiled, and their wives ravished. 17 Behold, I will stir up the Medes against them, which shall not regard silver; and as for gold, they shall not delight in it. 18 Their bows also shall dash the young men to pieces; and they shall have no pity on the fruit of the womb; their eyes shall not spare children.

13.6-18 The day of the Lord has an immediate meaning and a future fulfillment. The Medes are named in verse 17, for they were allied with the Babylonians. Babylon will eventually fall and not rise again Rev 14.8.

13.7 Melt. .fulfilled in Jer 50.43, Babylon was taken

by surprise on the night of Belshazzar's feast, hence sudden fainting and melting of hearts Dan 5.30.

13.10 Stars of heaven. .Is 34.4, Joel 2.10, Ez 32.7. Am 8.9, Rev 6.12-14.

13.11 Babylon's arrogance will be brought down, Dan 4.22, 30

13.17 Behold I will stir up the Medes. .at the Isaiah wrote this the Medes were subject to Assyria, subsequently Arbaces the satrap of Media revolted against the effeminate Sardanapalus the king of Assyria, destroyed Nineveh, and became king of Media in the ninth century BC. Jer 51.11 the Medes eventually destroy Babylon as well.

13.19-22 And Babylon, the glory of kingdoms, the beauty of the Chaldees' excellency, shall be as when God overthrew Sodom and Gomorrah. 20 It shall never be inhabited, neither shall it be dwelt in from generation to generation: neither shall the Arabian pitch tent there; neither shall the shepherds make their fold there. 21 But wild beasts of the desert shall lie there; and their houses shall be full of doleful creatures; and owls shall dwell there, and satyrs shall dance there. 22 And the wild beasts of the islands shall cry in their desolate houses, and dragons in their pleasant palaces: and her time is near to come, and her days shall not be prolonged.

13.19-22 The overthrow of Babylon is likened to the destruction of Sodom and Gomorrah. The desolation of Babylon shall be utter and complete. Isaiah closes this chapter by predicting that not only will Babylon be destroyed, but will never be rebuilt or inhabited by man or beast. Satyrs are believed by some to be demonic creatures, and can even be seen as some Islamic actions of today such as ISIS.

Chapter 14

14.1 For the Lord will have mercy on Jacob, and will yet choose Israel, and set them in their own land: and the strangers shall be joined with them, and they shall cleave to the house of Jacob.

14.1 This chapter is an elegiac lamentation for the two nations being judged by God, who God used to chastise His people. These two nations are Assyria and Babylon. The song has a taunting tone of victory for God's chosen people who eventually triumph over their tormentors. There is a sense of poetic justice as the voice of the oppressed lifts against the ones who now feel the grinding heel of God in their hour of righteous judgment. The same God who so easily swatted Assyria (Is 37.26), will deal with Babylon as easily as a man swats flies.

14.1 The present distress of Judah is not permanent. It will pass and the people will again possess their land.

14.2 And the people shall take them, and bring them to their place: and the house of Israel shall possess them in the land of the Lord for servants and handmaids:

and they shall take them captives, whose captives they were; and they shall rule over their oppressors.

14.2 God's people will one-day turn the tables and rule over their captors.

14.3 And it shall come to pass in the day that the Lord shall give thee rest from thy sorrow, and from thy fear, and from the hard bondage wherein thou wast made to serve,

14.3 Isaiah is never very far from alluding to the Millennial reign of the coming Messiah, here he promises rest from their oppression.

14.4-16 That thou shalt take up this proverb against the king of Babylon, and say, How hath the oppressor ceased! the golden city ceased! 5 The Lord hath broken the staff of the wicked, and the sceptre of the rulers. 6 He who smote the people in wrath with a continual stroke, he that ruled the nations in anger, is persecuted, and none hindereth. 7 The whole earth is at rest, and is quiet: they break forth into singing. 8 Yea, the fir trees rejoice at thee, and the cedars of Lebanon, saying, Since thou art laid down, no feller is come up against us. 9 Hell from beneath is moved for thee to meet thee at thy coming: it stirreth up the dead for thee, even all the chief ones of the earth; it hath raised up from their thrones all the kings of the nations. 10 All they shall speak and say unto thee, Art thou also become weak as we? art thou become like unto us? 11 Thy pomp is brought down to the grave, and the noise of thy viols: the worm is spread under thee, and the worms cover thee. 12 How art thou fallen from heaven, O Lucifer, son of the morning! how art thou cut down to the

ground, which didst weaken the nations! 13 For thou hast said in thine heart, I will ascend into heaven, I will exalt my throne above the stars of God: I will sit also upon the mount of the congregation, in the sides of the north: 14 I will ascend above the heights of the clouds; I will be like the most High. 15 Yet thou shalt be brought down to hell, to the sides of the pit. 16 They that see thee shall narrowly look upon thee, and consider thee, saying, Is this the man that made the earth to tremble, that did shake kingdoms;

14.4-14 Is one of the best-known passages of Isaiah's writings. Oriental lore use of proverbs is common. Mic 2.4, Hab 2.6 In this proverb the King of Babylon is seen representing much more than an earthly king. He represents Satan himself, who is the ruler of all earthly kingdoms. The slow pentameter of this song takes time to dwell on Hell being moved to meet Satan in verse 9. This causes them to break forth into song, verse 7. He (Satan) who felled the trees of Lebanon (verse 8), is now felled himself, and is vanquished. This is cause for celebration and songs of victory.

14.9 The scene now changes from earth to hell. Hell here is sheol, the abode of the dead.

14.10 The fall of Lucifer, which means light bearer, literally shakes hell (Ez 31.16). Lucifer is also called the morning star (planet Venus) that disappears when the sun rises. So Satan here is shown to disappear when the true "son" appears. Satan, the ruler of the kingdoms of this world met with earthly rulers in the north (Zaphon- the meeting hall of the Gods in ancient idol worship), in verse 13, to lay his diabolical plan to displace God. His fall and entrance into sheol is greeted with astonishment. He is seen in his natural state stripped of any illusion. The result is he is viewed with disdain and contempt (16)

14.11 Thy pomp. is brought to the grave and becomes maggot infested. Hence Lucifer's attempt to be the "day star" and replace Christ who is the true "bright and morning star" (Rev 22.16) fails.

14.17 That made the world as a wilderness, and destroyed the cities thereof; that opened not the house of his prisoners?

14.17 Opened not the house of his prisoners. . at this time Satan had the keys to hell, but when Jesus came He took them from Satan during the three days of His resurrection and now Christ holds them in His hand (Rev 1.18)

14.18-23 18 All the kings of the nations, even all of them, lie in glory, every one in his own house. 19 But thou art cast out of thy grave like an abominable branch, and as the raiment of those that are slain, thrust through with a sword, that go down to the stones of the pit; as a carcase trodden under feet. 20 Thou shalt not be joined with them in burial, because thou hast destroyed thy land, and slain thy people: the seed of evildoers shall never be renowned. 21 Prepare slaughter for his children for the iniquity of their fathers; that they do not rise, nor possess the land, nor fill the face of the world with cities. 22 For I will rise up against them, saith the Lord of hosts, and cut off from Babylon the name, and remnant, and son, and nephew, saith the Lord. 23 I will also make it a possession for the bittern, and pools of water: and I

will sweep it with the besom of destruction, saith the Lord of hosts.

14.18-23 Satan faces utter failure and expulsion. He will not simply be destroyed and forgotten, his judgment is certain and his fate sealed. His future is proclaimed along with the earthly nations. No one is exempt from God's judgment upon rebellion, no matter how high their spiritual status. Besom in verse 23 means broom and possibly refers to the coming judgment of Babylon 200 years in the future. God is fair and impartial in His righteous judgment.

14.24-27 The Lord of hosts hath sworn, saying, Surely as I have thought, so shall it come to pass; and as I have purposed, so shall it stand: 25 That I will break the Assyrian in my land, and upon my mountains tread him under foot: then shall his yoke depart from off them, and his burden depart from off their shoulders. 26 This is the purpose that is purposed upon the whole earth: and this is the hand that is stretched out upon all the nations. 27 For the Lord of hosts hath purposed, and who shall disannul it? and his hand is stretched out, and who shall turn it back?

14.24-27 The burden and pronouncement of judgment continues, now against Assyria. It is foretold God will break the Assyrian in His own land (God's land). This is fulfilled when the miraculous event of ch 37.36 occurs. God slays 185,000 Assyrians in one night literally upon the Judean mountains right outside the city of Jerusalem.

14.28-32 In the year that king Ahaz died was this burden. 29 Rejoice not thou, whole Palestina, because

the rod of him that smote thee is broken: for out of the serpent's root shall come forth a cockatrice, and his fruit shall be a fiery flying serpent. 30 And the firstborn of the poor shall feed, and the needy shall lie down in safety: and I will kill thy root with famine, and he shall slay thy remnant. 31 Howl, O gate; cry, O city; thou, whole Palestina, art dissolved: for there shall come from the north a smoke, and none shall be alone in his appointed times. 32 What shall one then answer the messengers of the nation? That the Lord hath founded Zion, and the poor of his people shall trust in it.

14.28-32 The prophet turns his burden of coming judgment now to Palestina (Philistines). In 727 BC he speaks this portion and foretells their demise. In 734 the Assyrians made Philistia a vassal state. The Philistines revolted against the Assyrians in 715 BC, but failed in their revolt. The Philistines then disappear from the pages of history forever. God's word was exact (30) "I will kill thy root. .and slay thy remnant." Thus ends Philistia, Satan's future, and all who rebel against the sovereignty of the Almighty.

Chapter 15

15.1-9 The burden of Moab. Because in the night Ar of Moab is laid waste, and brought to silence; because in the night Kir of Moab is laid waste, and brought to silence; 2 He is gone up to Bajith, and to Dibon, the high places, to weep: Moab shall howl over Nebo, and over Medeba: on all their heads shall be baldness, and every beard cut off. 3 In their streets they shall gird themselves with sackcloth: on the tops of their houses, and in their streets, every one shall howl, weeping abundantly. 4 And Heshbon shall cry, and Elealeh: their voice shall be heard even unto Jahaz: therefore the armed soldiers of Moab shall cry out; his life shall be grievous unto him. 5 My heart shall cry out for Moab; his fugitives shall flee unto Zoar, an heifer of three years old: for by the mounting up of Luhith with weeping shall they go it up; for in the way of Horonaim they shall raise up a cry of destruction. 6 For the waters of Nimrim shall be desolate: for the hay is withered away, the grass faileth, there is no green thing. 7 Therefore the abundance they have gotten, and that which they have laid up, shall they carry away to the brook of the willows. 8 For the cry is gone round about the borders of Moab; the howling thereof unto Eglaim, and the howling thereof unto

Beerelim. 9 For the waters of Dimon shall be full of blood: for I will bring more upon Dimon, lions upon him that escapeth of Moab, and upon the remnant of the land.

15.1-9 The eye of the prophet now turns to Moab. This is a natural sequence here because Moab joined with Philistia (Ch 14.28-32) in revolting against Assyria. Isaiah foretells the fall of the capital of Moab, their chief fortress, and a list of cities. These moments of prophecy give the details that can be traced exactly to prove the inerrancy of Isaiah and ultimately the God who speaks to Isaiah. One must wonder the significance of people fleeing to Zoar (5), the same city Lot fled to in his escape from the judgment upon Sodom.

15.5 The prophet is moved with pity for Moab. May the ministers of God always speak with tender sorrow, and never with satisfaction about destruction.

15.6 The grass faileth. .there was mourning at the complete and utter destruction, such as donning sackcloth, shaving hair, and plucking beards (Jer 48.37), but the final result was Moab also passes from the pages of history during the reign of Persia.

Chapter 16

16.1 Send ye the lamb to the ruler of the land from Sela to the wilderness, unto the mount of the daughter of Zion.

16.1 This chapter continues the prophecy against Moab. At this point the only hope Moab has is to make peace with Judah. "Send the lamb" means they are seeking peace and will pay tribute to the dynasty of David. David is of their common ancestry though Ruth. From Sela refers to the area of Petra identifying them clearly. Moab had once paid tribute of 100,000 lambs (2 K 3.4-5), but had stopped when Ahab died. They are now willing to resume their tribute. David probably instituted this in 2 Sam 8.2.

16.2-5 For it shall be, that, as a wandering bird cast out of the nest, so the daughters of Moab shall be at the fords of Arnon. 3 Take counsel, execute judgment; make thy shadow as the night in the midst of the noonday; hide the outcasts; bewray not him that wandereth. 4 Let mine outcasts dwell with thee, Moab; be thou a covert to them from the face of the spoiler: for the extortioner is at an end, the spoiler ceaseth, the oppressors are consumed out of the land. 5 And in

mercy shall the throne be established: and he shall sit upon it in truth in the tabernacle of David, judging, and seeking judgment, and hasting righteousness.

16.2-5 When the ax falls and judgment comes Moab pleads for mercy upon the outcasts that escape. They will appeal to the mercy of the tabernacle of David.

16.6-8 We have heard of the pride of Moab; he is very proud: even of his haughtiness, and his pride, and his wrath: but his lies shall not be so. 7 Therefore shall Moab howl for Moab, every one shall howl: for the foundations of Kirhareseth shall ye mourn; surely they are stricken. 8 For the fields of Heshbon languish, and the vine of Sibmah: the lords of the heathen have broken down the principal plants thereof, they are come even unto Jazer, they wandered through the wilderness: her branches are stretched out, they are gone over the sea.

16.6-8 The pride of Moab. .pride goeth before destruction. .so Moab shall fall. The alluding to grapes and vines speak of God withholding help.

16.9-14 Therefore I will bewail with the weeping of Jazer the vine of Sibmah: I will water thee with my tears, O Heshbon, and Elealeh: for the shouting for thy summer fruits and for thy harvest is fallen. 10 And gladness is taken away, and joy out of the plentiful field; and in the vineyards there shall be no singing, neither shall there be shouting: the treaders shall tread out no wine in their presses; I have made their vintage shouting to cease. 11 Wherefore my bowels shall sound like an harp for Moab, and mine inward parts for Kirharesh. 12 And it shall come to pass, when

it is seen that Moab is weary on the high place, that he shall come to his sanctuary to pray; but he shall not prevail. 13 This is the word that the Lord hath spoken concerning Moab since that time. 14 But now the Lord hath spoken, saying, Within three years, as the years of an hireling, and the glory of Moab shall be contemned, with all that great multitude; and the remnant shall be very small and feeble.

16.9-14 The glory of Moab will end. .even though Moab deserves the coming judgment, the prophet Isaiah weeps over their calamity. He feels it deeply in his inward man (my bowels shall sound like a harp), my heart shall cry out for Moab (15.5).

16.10 Gladness is taken away. .the joy of harvest has ceased; Isaiah is deeply moved concerning this tragedy.

16.11 Bowels. .this always refers to the deepest inward feelings, (Jer 48.36).

16.12-14 The epitaph of Moab. .prayers are not heard; within three years Moab is contemned (despised). Isaiah is literally preaching the funeral of a once proud nation that has died in ignominy.

Chapter 17

17.1-5 The burden of Damascus. Behold, Damascus is taken away from being a city, and it shall be a ruinous heap. 2 The cities of Aroer are forsaken: they shall be for flocks, which shall lie down, and none shall make them afraid. 3 The fortress also shall cease from Ephraim, and the kingdom from Damascus, and the remnant of Syria: they shall be as the glory of the children of Israel, saith the Lord of hosts. 4 And in that day it shall come to pass, that the glory of Jacob shall be made thin, and the fatness of his flesh shall wax lean. 5 And it shall be as when the harvestman gathereth the corn, and reapeth the ears with his arm; and it shall be as he that gathereth ears in the valley of Rephaim.

17.1 The Lord now directs Isaiah's prophetic gaze to the nations around Israel. This is one more reason Isaiah is considered a major prophet. His view and scope of prophecy is broad and far reaching. The next few chapters focus on Damascus, Ethiopia, Egypt then returns to Babylon again. (Chapters 17-21)

17.1-5 Again Isaiah speaks out of a burden. It saddens the prophet to see the ruin and destruction of sin. He forecasts a ruinous heap, loss of flocks (wealth), and the effect reaches into the people of God. So often the judgment of God upon a nation or people affect those around them by proxy. In this setting Tiglath-pileser destroys Damascus in 732 BC. The overflow and cause and effect bleeds over to Israel and Judah. The valley of Rephaim was renowned for much harvest, but is singled out to show there will be minimal returns when God speaks their judgment. This should always be a reminder that God controls ever the cycles of nature.

17.3 Fortress shall cease. .fulfilled in 2 K 16.9.

17.5 The harvest of Samaria fulfilled in 2 K 18.9-11.

17.6-8 Yet gleaning grapes shall be left in it, as the shaking of an olive tree, two or three berries in the top of the uppermost bough, four or five in the outmost fruitful branches thereof, saith the Lord God of Israel. 7 At that day shall a man look to his Maker, and his eyes shall have respect to the Holy One of Israel.8 And he shall not look to the altars, the work of his hands, neither shall respect that which his fingers have made, either the groves, or the images.

17.6-8 The judgment has the desired effect as men turn back to God and away from the gods of their hands. The groves represent a symbolical tree often found in Assyrian inscriptions that represent the hosts of heaven. Saba represents Ashteroth the queen of heaven, as Bel or Baal represents the king of heaven.

17.9-11 In that day shall his strong cities be as a forsaken bough, and an uppermost branch, which

they left because of the children of Israel: and there shall be desolation. 10 Because thou hast forgotten the God of thy salvation, and hast not been mindful of the rock of thy strength, therefore shalt thou plant pleasant plants, and shalt set it with strange slips: 11 In the day shalt thou make thy plant to grow, and in the morning shalt thou make thy seed to flourish: but the harvest shall be a heap in the day of grief and of desperate sorrow.

17.9-11 The strong cities will not be strong against the Almighty. Mighty Damascus, which was powerful when warring against earthly foes, is weak and impotent against a single word from God. After the destruction, even an attempt to again restore the prosperity will be thwarted by God's word that endures forever; the harvest will be a heap in the day of grief.

17.12-14 Woe to the multitude of many people, which make a noise like the noise of the seas; and to the rushing of nations, that make a rushing like the rushing of mighty waters! 13 The nations shall rush like the rushing of many waters: but God shall rebuke them, and they shall flee far off, and shall be chased as the chaff of the mountains before the wind, and like a rolling thing before the whirlwind. 14 And behold at eveningtide trouble; and before the morning he is not. This is the portion of them that spoil us, and the lot of them that rob us.

17.12-14 The people of God are encouraged by Isaiah. Though many waters (people) rage and boast and try to rush against Israel and Judah, God simply rebukes them and they are chased away as chaff before the wind. This is the portion of the ones who spoil and rob God's people. Again Isaiah reassures a fearful nation, trust in the Lord. God is the answer for every looming challenge and nothing is even remotely difficult for God.

Chapter 18

18.1-7 Woe to the land shadowing with wings, which is beyond the rivers of Ethiopia: 2 That sendeth ambassadors by the sea, even in vessels of bulrushes upon the waters, saying, Go, ye swift messengers, to a nation scattered and peeled, to a people terrible from their beginning hitherto; a nation meted out and trodden down, whose land the rivers have spoiled! 3 All ye inhabitants of the world, and dwellers on the earth, see ye, when he lifteth up an ensign on the mountains; and when he bloweth a trumpet, hear ye. 4 For so the Lord said unto me, I will take my rest, and I will consider in my dwelling place like a clear heat upon herbs, and like a cloud of dew in the heat of harvest. 5 For afore the harvest, when the bud is perfect, and the sour grape is ripening in the flower, he shall both cut off the sprigs with pruning hooks, and take away and cut down the branches. 6 They shall be left together unto the fowls of the mountains, and to the beasts of the earth: and the fowls shall summer upon them, and all the beasts of the earth shall winter upon them. 7 In that time shall the present be brought unto the Lord of hosts of a people scattered and peeled, and from a people terrible from their beginning hitherto; a nation meted out and trodden under foot, whose

land the rivers have spoiled, to the place of the name of the Lord of hosts, the mount Zion.

18.1-7 Isaiah is still viewing the nations surrounding Israel and foretelling their coming judgment. His prophetic eye now focuses on Egypt and Ethiopia. This would be the descendants of the Cushites, sometimes referred to as the Nubians. These Ethiopians wanted to make a pact with Judah against Assyria. Isaiah warned against this alliance. Isaiah had seen in the spiritual realm that Assyria was in God's time clock to bring judgment on other nations before their own destruction. Ethiopia had overrun Egypt in 715BC and would rule them in Egypt's 25th dynasty until 701BC, when Sennacherib of Assyria crushed them at El Tekeh.

18.2 Vessels of bulrushes. .these are Papyrus boats, a miniature was used for Moses in Ex 2.3. To a people terrible. .the Ethopians were famed for their warlike prowess.

18.7 Shall the present be brought to the Lord. .Zech 14.16, in the millennial reign of Christ, all nations will do homage to the Lord. Again Isaiah asserts that God is in full control of every nation and every person on planet earth. God can and does foretell each nation and how their future unfolds. Acts 15.18 known unto God are all His works from the beginning of the world.

Chapter 19

19.1. The burden of Egypt. Behold, the Lord rideth upon a swift cloud, and shall come into Egypt: and the idols of Egypt shall be moved at his presence, and the heart of Egypt shall melt in the midst of it.

19.1 The time has arrived to settle an old score with an old enemy- Egypt, and God uncharacteristically arrives on a swift cloud. Isaiah brings a message of both judgment and hope.

19.2 And I will set the Egyptians against the Egyptians: and they shall fight every one against his brother, and every one against his neighbour; city against city, and kingdom against kingdom.

19.2 Egyptian against Egyptian. .civil war came to Egypt in 671 BC, and the land is conquered by Esar-haddon of Assyria.

19.3 And the spirit of Egypt shall fail in the midst thereof; and I will destroy the counsel thereof: and they shall seek to the idols, and to the charmers, and to them that have familiar spirits, and to the wizards.

19.3 Idols. .charmers. .The gods and religion of Egypt will prove worthless when the true God stands to speak judgment.

19.4 And the Egyptians will I give over into the hand of a cruel lord; and a fierce king shall rule over them, saith the Lord, the Lord of hosts.

19.4 Cruel lord. .Assyrian overlords who dominated Egypt for 20 years

19.5-10 And the waters shall fail from the sea, and the river shall be wasted and dried up. 6 And they shall turn the rivers far away; and the brooks of defence shall be emptied and dried up: the reeds and flags shall wither. 7 The paper reeds by the brooks, by the mouth of the brooks, and every thing sown by the brooks, shall wither, be driven away, and be no more. 8 The fishers also shall mourn, and all they that cast angle into the brooks shall lament, and they that spread nets upon the waters shall languish. 9 Moreover they that work in fine flax, and they that weave networks, shall be confounded. 10 And they shall be broken in the purposes thereof, all that make sluices and ponds for fish.

19.5-10 The judgment of God strikes at the strength of a nation when it is sent forth. When Moab is judged it is her fertile land that is attacked (16.10-11), which was her noted strength. For Egypt the Nile River had been her strength for centuries, so God shows his power by striking her most dominant asset.

19.11-18 Surely the princes of Zoan are fools, the counsel of the wise counsellors of Pharaoh is become

brutish: how say ye unto Pharaoh, I am the son of the wise, the son of ancient kings? 12 Where are they? where are thy wise men? and let them tell thee now, and let them know what the Lord of hosts hath purposed upon Egypt. 13 The princes of Zoan are become fools, the princes of Noph are deceived; they have also seduced Egypt, even they that are the stay of the tribes thereof. 14 The Lord hath mingled a perverse spirit in the midst thereof: and they have caused Egypt to err in every work thereof, as a drunken man staggereth in his vomit. 15 Neither shall there be any work for Egypt, which the head or tail, branch or rush, may do. 16 In that day shall Egypt be like unto women: and it shall be afraid and fear because of the shaking of the hand of the Lord of hosts, which he shaketh over it. 17 And the land of Judah shall be a terror unto Egypt, every one that maketh mention thereof shall be afraid in himself, because of the counsel of the Lord of hosts, which he hath determined against it. 18 In that day shall five cities in the land of Egypt speak the language of Canaan, and swear to the Lord of hosts; one shall be called, The city of destruction.

19.11-18 The wisdom of Egypt is shown to be foolhardy and vain. God controls even the wisdom of the world. There is no limit to the reach of God. (16), like a woman. .ancient cultures described defeated foes as women, so here Isaiah under the inspiration of the Almighty taunts Egypt as she has taunted others. One of God's eternal principals is we reap what we sow. It is more than poetic justice, it is reaping the same harvest we inflict upon others. (Matt 7.1-2, Gal 6.7-9)

19.18 Egypt will be so humbled they will speak Hebrew, the language of their weakest neighbor.

19.19-21 In that day shall there be an altar to the Lord in the midst of the land of Egypt, and a pillar at the border thereof to the Lord. 20 And it shall be for a sign and for a witness unto the Lord of hosts in the land of Egypt: for they shall cry unto the Lord because of the oppressors, and he shall send them a saviour, and a great one, and he shall deliver them. 21 And the Lord shall be known to Egypt, and the Egyptians shall know the Lord in that day, and shall do sacrifice and oblation; yea, they shall vow a vow unto the Lord, and perform it.

19.19-21 Altar to the Lord. .the coming of Messiah will not be national to Israel alone, it will be global and Israel's God will reign supreme over all false Gods. Egypt will bow the knee to Jesus Christ (Phil 2.10)

19.22-25 And the Lord shall smite Egypt: he shall smite and heal it: and they shall return even to the Lord, and he shall be intreated of them, and shall heal them. 23 In that day shall there be a highway out of Egypt to Assyria, and the Assyrian shall come into Egypt, and the Egyptian into Assyria, and the Egyptians shall serve with the Assyrians. 24 In that day shall Israel be the third with Egypt and with Assyria, even a blessing in the midst of the land: 25 Whom the Lord of hosts shall bless, saying, Blessed be Egypt my people, and Assyria the work of my hands, and Israel mine inheritance.

19.22-25 In that day. shall be a highway. .Today, two and a half millenniums later, this may not be a glaring statement, but when spoken in the eighth century BC, it must have seemed impossible. To proclaim this triumvirate would coexist, and be at peace, must have seemed surreal at that time. The union of Israel, Assyria and Egypt joined in peace and unity would take nothing less that the mighty hand of God. Isaiah was boldly declaring a coming world like nothing any of them had ever seen or could imagine. Truly God is able to do exceeding abundantly above all that we can ask or think (Eph 3.20)

Chapter 20

20.1 In the year that Tartan came unto Ashdod, (when Sargon the king of Assyria sent him,) and fought against Ashdod, and took it;

20.1 Tartan. .was the general of Sargon the king of Assyria (2 K 18.17). Tartan is an Akkadian military title. This general stamped out the Philistine rebellion (Is14.29-32)

20.2-6 At the same time spake the Lord by Isaiah the son of Amoz, saying, Go and loose the sackcloth from off thy loins, and put off thy shoe from thy foot. And he did so, walking naked and barefoot. 3 And the Lord said, Like as my servant Isaiah hath walked naked and barefoot three years for a sign and wonder upon Egypt and upon Ethiopia; 4 So shall the king of Assyria lead away the Egyptians prisoners, and the Ethiopians captives, young and old, naked and barefoot, even with their buttocks uncovered, to the shame of Egypt. 5 And they shall be afraid and ashamed of Ethiopia their expectation, and of Egypt their glory. 6 And the inhabitant of this isle shall say in that day, Behold, such is our expectation, whither we flee for help

to be delivered from the king of Assyria: and how shall we escape?

20.2-6 Possibly Isaiah was to dress like an exile. This was the way an exile would dress. Isaiah was informing the nation that to align themselves with any surrounding nations would only bring hardship. They should trust completely in the Lord. Micah a contemporary of Isaiah also walked around like this (Mi 1.8) This was Isaiah's only symbolic act. Later prophets like Jeremiah and Ezekiel would use this technique more.

20.4 Egypt and Ethiopia. .Ethiopia would be taken captive by Assyria, which was known for stripping its captives naked and sometimes even peeling their skin of while they were still alive. For three years Isaiah provided a living glimpse of what tragedy awaited those who allied themselves with earthly powers. Israel's hope should always rest in the one true and living God.

Chapter 21

21.1 The burden of the desert of the sea. As whirlwinds in the south pass through; so it cometh from the desert, from a terrible land.

21.1 The oracle concerning the desert of the sea. .this unique and unusual title immediately stands out. The possibilities for this title are several. In prophecy sea represents people. This chapter and chapter 22 are a tetralogy of massas in symbolic and poetic form. A tetralogy is a series of four connected works. So here Isaiah beautifully and eloquently writes in imagery the repeated vision of the fall and demise of Babylon. The once populated land (sea) will become a desert (exiles taken away).

21.2-4 A grievous vision is declared unto me; the treacherous dealer dealeth treacherously, and the spoiler spoileth. Go up, O Elam: besiege, O Media; all the sighing thereof have I made to cease. 3 Therefore are my loins filled with pain: pangs have taken hold upon me, as the pangs of a woman that travaileth: I was bowed down at the hearing of it; I was dismayed at the seeing of it. 4 My heart panted, fearfulness affrighted me: the night of my pleasure hath he turned into fear unto me.

21.2-4 Isaiah experiences pain, sadness, and misery at the vision of unfolding horror of the first massa. Though Babylon is Judah's oppressor, the prophet finds no delight in her destruction.

21.5-10 Prepare the table, watch in the watchtower, eat, drink: arise, ye princes, and anoint the shield. 6 For thus hath the Lord said unto me, Go, set a watchman, let him declare what he seeth. 7 And he saw a chariot with a couple of horsemen, a chariot of asses, and a chariot of camels; and he hearkened diligently with much heed: 8 And he cried, A lion: My lord, I stand continually upon the watchtower in the daytime, and I am set in my ward whole nights: 9 And, behold, here cometh a chariot of men, with a couple of horsemen. And he answered and said, Babylon is fallen, is fallen; and all the graven images of her gods he hath broken unto the ground. 10 O my threshing, and the corn of my floor: that which I have heard of the Lord of hosts, the God of Israel, have I declared unto you.

21.5-10 In the second massa Isaiah assumes the role in the vision as though he were the watchman of the city. By doing this, his vantage point is easier explained. He sees chariots of asses, camels, riders, and even lions attacking. As watchman he signals the danger to the inhabitants below.

21.11-17 The burden of Dumah. He calleth to me out of Seir, Watchman, what of the night? Watchman, what of the night? 12 The watchman said, The morning cometh, and also the night: if ye will enquire, enquire ye: return, come. 13 The burden upon Arabia. In the forest in Arabia shall ye lodge, O ye travelling companies of Dedanim. 14 The inhabitants of the

land of Tema brought water to him that was thirsty, they prevented with their bread him that fled. 15 For they fled from the swords, from the drawn sword, and from the bent bow, and from the grievousness of war. 16 For thus hath the Lord said unto me, Within a year, according to the years of an hireling, and all the glory of Kedar shall fail: 17 And the residue of the number of archers, the mighty men of the children of Kedar, shall be diminished: for the Lord God of Israel hath spoken it.

21.11-17 Is the third massa in the tetralogy. After the warning of the previous second massa of the tetralogy, the inhabitants are desperate for news of the vision of approaching disaster. Much like an unfolding drama in a play on a national scale, Isaiah relates what he sees. He relates morning and night are coming (the genesis and finish of the vision). There will be bows and arrows, swords, and grievous war. Within a year of this vision Babylon's mighty men and her archer's of war will be history. Chapter 24 is the fourth and final massa of this poetic tetralogy.

Chapter 22

22.1 The burden of the valley of vision. What aileth thee now, that thou art wholly gone up to the housetops?

22.1 The fourth and final massa of this tetralogy concerns Jerusalem and her perspective of the previous three massas. It is possible that Isaiah looked out the window of his personal residence (which was in the lower part of the city), and saw the mount of Olives (300 ft. high) to the east, and mount Zion to the south and so speaks "the oracle of the valley of vision." A valley is a deep, still, solitary place, cut off and shut in by mountains. And thus Jerusalem was an enclosed place, hidden and shut off from the world, which Jehovah had chosen as the place in which to show to His prophets the mysteries of His government of the world. And upon this prophet's sacred city the judgment of Jehovah was about to fall; and the announcement of the judgment upon it is placed among the oracles concerning the nations of the world. We may see from this, that at the time when this prophecy was uttered, the attitude of Jerusalem was so worldly and heathenish, that it called forth this dark, nocturnal threat, which is penetrated by not a single glimmer of promise.

22.2-3 Thou that art full of stirs, a tumultuous city, joyous city: thy slain men are not slain with the sword, nor dead in battle. 3 All thy rulers are fled together, they are bound by the archers: all that are found in thee are bound together, which have fled from far.

22.2-3 A joyous city. . because King Hezekiah had averted war by paying tribute (2K 18.14-16 And Hezekiah king of Judah sent to the king of Assyria to Lachish, saying, I have offended; return from me: that which thou puttest on me will I bear. And the king of Assyria appointed unto Hezekiah king of Judah three hundred talents of silver and thirty talents of gold. And Hezekiah gave him all the silver that was found in the house of the LORD, and in the treasures of the king's house. At that time did Hezekiah cut off the gold from the doors of the temple of the LORD, and from the pillars which Hezekiah king of Judah had overlaid, and gave it to the king of Assyria.)

22.4 Therefore said I, Look away from me; I will weep bitterly, labour not to comfort me, because of the spoiling of the daughter of my people.

22.4 Look away from me; I will weep bitterly. .Isaiah's distress over the fall of Jerusalem in this vision.

22.5-14 For it is a day of trouble, and of treading down, and of perplexity by the Lord God of hosts in the valley of vision, breaking down the walls, and of crying to the mountains. 6 And Elam bare the quiver with chariots of men and horsemen, and Kir uncovered the shield. 7 And it shall come to pass, that thy choicest valleys shall be full of chariots, and the horsemen shall set themselves in array at the gate. 8 And he discovered

the covering of Judah, and thou didst look in that day to the armour of the house of the forest. 9 Ye have seen also the breaches of the city of David, that they are many: and ye gathered together the waters of the lower pool. 10 And ye have numbered the houses of Jerusalem, and the houses have ye broken down to fortify the wall. 11 Ye made also a ditch between the two walls for the water of the old pool: but ye have not looked unto the maker thereof, neither had respect unto him that fashioned it long ago. 12 And in that day did the Lord God of hosts call to weeping, and to mourning, and to baldness, and to girding with sackcloth: 13 And behold joy and gladness, slaying oxen, and killing sheep, eating flesh, and drinking wine: let us eat and drink; for to morrow we shall die. 14 And it was revealed in mine ears by the Lord of hosts, Surely this iniquity shall not be purged from you till ye die, saith the Lord God of hosts.

22.5-14 While Judah celebrated their narrow escape from Assyria, the prophet warns them of their own iniquities and pending judgment. Isaiah is bewildered with their celebrations upon the housetops from where they saw the retreating enemy. He refers to the arsenal in the house of the forest where their weapons were kept (1K 7.2, 10.17,21), and warns that the storm that was engulfing the whole area would also dump impending doom on Judah as well. Their weapons will not save them; their hope lies in turning to the Lord. Isaiah mentions the actions of King Hezekiah concerning the conduits of the water. This was a major engineering project to protect Jerusalem's water supply in the event of a siege. The king diverted the water of the Gihon Spring into a channel (2Ch 32.2-4). He followed this with building an aqueduct that brought the same water to the pool of Siloam in Jerusalem. This was accomplished by two teams digging toward each other and meeting in the middle (2K 20.20, 2 Ch 32.2-4). King Hezekiah also constructed Hezekiah's pool (2 K 18.17)

22.13-14 Let us eat and drink; for to morrow we shall die. .this attitude so angered God he told Isaiah to inform his people. .Surely this iniquity shall not be purged from you till ye die.

22.15-21 Thus saith the Lord God of hosts, Go, get thee unto this treasurer, even unto Shebna, which is over the house, and say, 16 What hast thou here? and whom hast thou here, that thou hast hewed thee out a sepulchre here, as he that heweth him out a sepulchre on high, and that graveth an habitation for himself in a rock? 17 Behold, the Lord will carry thee away with a mighty captivity, and will surely cover thee. 18 He will surely violently turn and toss thee like a ball into a large country: there shalt thou die, and there the chariots of thy glory shall be the shame of thy lord's house. 19 And I will drive thee from thy station, and from thy state shall he pull thee down. 20 And it shall come to pass in that day, that I will call my servant Eliakim the son of Hilkiah: 21 And I will clothe him with thy robe, and strengthen him with thy girdle, and I will commit thy government into his hand: and he shall be a father to the inhabitants of Jerusalem, and to the house of Judah.

22.15-21 Shebna. .he seems to be the leader of the pro-Egyptian faction of Jerusalem. Shebna had ordered a large sepulcher to be built in his own honor, assuming to be secure in his high position. Isaiah predicts he will be demoted and will die a pauper in a foreign country.

Shebna is replaced by Eliakim (2K 18.18). God declares he will toss Shebna like a ball into a large country where he will die.

22.22-25 And the key of the house of David will I lay upon his shoulder; so he shall open, and none shall shut; and he shall shut, and none shall open. 23 And I will fasten him as a nail in a sure place; and he shall be for a glorious throne to his father's house. 24 And they shall hang upon him all the glory of his father's house, the offspring and the issue, all vessels of small quantity, from the vessels of cups, even to all the vessels of flagons. 25 In that day, saith the Lord of hosts, shall the nail that is fastened in the sure place be removed, and be cut down, and fall; and the burden that was upon it shall be cut off: for the Lord hath spoken it.

22.22 And the key of the house of David will I lay upon his shoulder. . The power of the keys consisted not only in the supervision of the royal chambers, but also in the decision who was and who was not to be received into the king's service. There is a resemblance, therefore, to the giving of the keys of the kingdom of heaven to Peter by Christ in the New Testament (Mt 16.19). These keys given to Peter, were used to open the door of the church in Acts. 2.1-42, when the New Testament Church was born.

22.20-25 And it shall come to pass in that day, that I will call my servant Eliakim. .after disposing of Shebna, God promotes Eliakim, who God refers to as a nail in a sure place, upon which God will hang all the glory of his father's house. Furthermore, Eliakim is given the Key to the house of David. The dying echo of prophecy from this fourth massa of the tetralogy, the oracle of the valley of vision, assures the continuation of the house of David! Again, Isaiah sees the coming messiah (Jesus) through the smoke and haze of centuries, through the march or armies, and the ebb and flow of world powers. Thus the "massa of the valley of vision" became a memorial of mercy to Israel when it looked back to its past history: but when it looked into the future, it was still a mirror of wrath.

Chapter 23

23.1-3 The burden of Tyre. Howl, ye ships of Tarshish; for it is laid waste, so that there is no house, no entering in: from the land of Chittim it is revealed to them. 2 Be still, ye inhabitants of the isle; thou whom the merchants of Zidon, that pass over the sea, have replenished. 3 And by great waters the seed of Sihor, the harvest of the river, is her revenue; and she is a mart of nations.

23.1-3 The all seeing eye of God now directs the attention of Isaiah to Tyre. In this section of looking at the nations of the world around Jerusalem, Isaiah had begun with Babylon, the political power. He now turns to the commercial power, Tyre and Sidon. Babylon was the city of the imperial power of the world, Tyre, the city of the commerce of the world. Babylon was the center of the greatest land power; Tyre of the greatest maritime power. Babylon ruled by might, Tyre ruled by materialism. This chapter gives an account both of the desolation and restoration of Tyre, an ancient city of Phoenicia. Its desolation is described as so complete, that a house was not left in it (Isa 23:1), and the inhabitants of it were gone. The inhabitants would be replenished after 70 years and it would again become a trading center of nations (Isa 23:2).

23.4-5 Be thou ashamed, O Zidon: for the sea hath spoken, even the strength of the sea, saying, I travail not, nor bring forth children, neither do I nourish up young men, nor bring up virgins. 5 As at the report concerning Egypt, so shall they be sorely pained at the report of Tyre.

23.4-5 Be thou ashamed, O Zidon. . Sidon, the ancestress of Canaan, must hear with overwhelming shame how Tyre mourns the loss of her daughters, and complains that, robbed as she has been of her children, she is like a barren women. For the war to have murdered her young men and maidens, was exactly the same as if she had never given birth to them or brought them up.

23.6-9 Pass ye over to Tarshish; howl, ye inhabitants of the isle. 7 Is this your joyous city, whose antiquity is of ancient days? her own feet shall carry her afar off to sojourn. 8 Who hath taken this counsel against Tyre, the crowning city, whose merchants are princes, whose traffickers are the honourable of the earth? 9 The Lord of hosts hath purposed it, to stain the pride of all glory, and to bring into contempt all the honourable of the earth.

23.6-9 Pass ye over to Tarshish; howl. . The inhabitants of Tyre, who desired to escape from death or exile, are obliged to take refuge in the colonies, and the farther off the better.

23.9 To stain the pride of all glory. .Tyre being proud of its riches, the extent of its commerce, and the multitude of its inhabitants, God was resolved, who sets himself against the proud, to abase them; to pollute the glorious things they were proud of; to deal with them as with polluted things; to trample upon them:

23.10 Pass through thy land as a river, O daughter of Tarshish: there is no more strength.

23.10 When Tyre falls all her colonies are liberated and flow over the land like the Nile River.

23.11-18 He stretched out his hand over the sea, he shook the kingdoms: the Lord hath given a commandment against the merchant city, to destroy the strong holds thereof. 12 And he said, Thou shalt no more rejoice, O thou oppressed virgin, daughter of Zidon: arise, pass over to Chittim; there also shalt thou have no rest. 13 Behold the land of the Chaldeans; this people was not, till the Assyrian founded it for them that dwell in the wilderness: they set up the towers thereof, they raised up the palaces thereof; and he brought it to ruin. 14 Howl, ye ships of Tarshish: for your strength is laid waste. 15 And it shall come to pass in that day, that Tyre shall be forgotten seventy years, according to the days of one king: after the end of seventy years shall Tyre sing as an harlot. 16 Take an harp, go about the city, thou harlot that hast been forgotten; make sweet melody, sing many songs, that thou mayest be remembered. 17 And it shall come to pass after the end of seventy years, that the Lord will visit Tyre, and she shall turn to her hire, and shall commit fornication with all the kingdoms of the world upon the face of the earth. 18 And her merchandise and her hire shall be holiness to the Lord: it shall not be treasured nor laid up; for her merchandise shall be

for them that dwell before the Lord, to eat sufficiently, and for durable clothing.

23.11-18 He stretched out his hand over the sea, he shook the kingdoms. .God controls every thing on both land and sea. There is no escape when he rises to pronounce judgment. The judgment of Tyre illustrated to God's people "his arm is not short." The greatest maritime nation in the history of the world would shrivel and dry up at the words of God's spokesman; Isaiah. Then in 70 years when all seemed lost, one word from God and voila the city rises again like a jilted lover who had been cast aside. She is like a bayadere or troubadour going through the streets with song and guitar, and bringing her charms into notice again. She is restored, again becoming rich and desired by the leading world nations. This ends the oracle of Tyre, and the surrounding nations. Isaiah now moves on to earth's future and the imminent invasion of Assyria.

Chapter 24

24.1 Behold, the Lord maketh the earth empty, and maketh it waste, and turneth it upside down, and scattereth abroad the inhabitants thereof.

24.1 This section of Isaiah (24-27) is sometimes called the little apocalypse. The word apocalyptic comes from the Greek word meaning to reveal or uncover. These chapters present universal judgment and universal blessing. It is thoroughly characteristic of Isaiah, that the beginning of this prophecy, places us at once in the very midst of the catastrophe, and condenses the contents of the judgment into a few rapid, vigorous, vivid, and comprehensive clauses. This chapter contains a prophecy of calamities that should come upon the whole world, and the inhabitants of it, for their sins; of the visitation of the kings of the earth; and of the appearance of Christ in his glory and majesty.

24.1 "Turneth it upside down." This means to change the face of it completely. Could this refer to future nuclear war, that it has not the form it had, and does not look like what it was, but is reduced to its original chaos.

24.2 And it shall be, as with the people, so with the priest; as with the servant, so with his master; as with the maid, so with her mistress; as with the buyer, so with the seller; as with the lender, so with the borrower; as with the taker of usury, so with the giver of usury to him.

24.2 "As with people." There will be no distinction with any of the people, all will be caught in the disaster.

24.3 The land shall be utterly emptied, and utterly spoiled: for the Lord hath spoken this word.

24.3 The land shall be utterly emptied, and utterly spoiled,. . Entirely emptied of its inhabitants, and wholly spoiled of its riches and substance. It is a judgment, which embraces all, without distinction of rank and condition; and it is a universal one, not merely throughout the whole of the land of Israel.

24.4-9 The earth mourneth and fadeth away, the world languisheth and fadeth away, the haughty people of the earth do languish. 5 The earth also is defiled under the inhabitants thereof; because they have transgressed the laws, changed the ordinance, broken the everlasting covenant. 6 Therefore hath the curse devoured the earth, and they that dwell therein are desolate: therefore the inhabitants of the earth are burned, and few men left. 7 The new wine mourneth, the vine languisheth, all the merryhearted do sigh. 8 The mirth of tabrets ceaseth, the noise of them that rejoice endeth, the joy of the harp ceaseth. 9 They shall not drink wine with a song; strong drink shall be bitter to them that drink it.

24.4-9 The earth mourneth, and fadeth away,. . It mourns, because of its inhabitants being destroyed; and it fades away, because stripped of its wealth and riches. The inhabitants of it are like a sick man, that is so faint and feeble that he cannot stand, but totters and falls; and like the leaves of trees and flowers of the fields, whose strength and beauty are gone, and fade and fall. Broken the everlasting covenant. . the new covenant, which is to last to the end of time. Wine and music, symbolic of happiness, ceases in the midst of the great world judgment.

24.10-12 The city of confusion is broken down: every house is shut up, that no man may come in. 11 There is a crying for wine in the streets; all joy is darkened, the mirth of the land is gone. 12 In the city is left desolation, and the gate is smitten with destruction.

24.10-12 City of confusion. .Jerusalem, in the midst of judgment. The state of things produced by the catastrophe is compared to the olive-beating, which fetches down what fruit was left at the general picking, and to the gleaning of the grapes after the vintage has been fully gathered in.

24.13-18 When thus it shall be in the midst of the land among the people, there shall be as the shaking of an olive tree, and as the gleaning grapes when the vintage is done. 14 They shall lift up their voice, they shall sing for the majesty of the Lord, they shall cry aloud from the sea. 15 Wherefore glorify ye the Lord in the fires, even the name of the Lord God of Israel in the isles of the sea. 16 From the uttermost part of the earth have we heard songs, even glory to the righteous. But I said, My leanness, my leanness, woe unto me! the

treacherous dealers have dealt treacherously; yea, the treacherous dealers have dealt very treacherously. 17 Fear, and the pit, and the snare, are upon thee, O inhabitant of the earth. 18 And it shall come to pass, that he who fleeth from the noise of the fear shall fall into the pit; and he that cometh up out of the midst of the pit shall be taken in the snare: for the windows from on high are open, and the foundations of the earth do shake.

24.13-18 There is now a church there refined by the judgment, and rejoicing in its Apostolic calling to the whole world. "They will lift up their voice, and exult; for the majesty of Jehovah they shout from the sea: therefore praise ye Jehovah in the lands of the sun, in the islands of the sea the name of Jehovah the God of Israel." The ground and subject of the rejoicing is "the majesty of Jehovah, the fact that Jehovah had shown Himself so majestic in judgment and mercy. *From the uttermost part of the earth.* . . . The reference is to the church of righteous men, whose faith has endured the fire of the judgment of wrath. In response to its summons to the praise of Jehovah, they answer it in songs from the border of the earth. It is possible that this also refers to some kind of nuclear holocaust.

24.19-23 The earth is utterly broken down, the earth is clean dissolved, the earth is moved exceedingly. 20 The earth shall reel to and fro like a drunkard, and shall be removed like a cottage; and the transgression thereof shall be heavy upon it; and it shall fall, and not rise again. 21 And it shall come to pass in that day, that the Lord shall punish the host of the high ones that are on high, and the kings of the earth upon the earth. 22 And they shall be gathered together, as prisoners are

gathered in the pit, and shall be shut up in the prison, and after many days shall they be visited. 23 Then the moon shall be confounded, and the sun ashamed, when the Lord of hosts shall reign in mount Zion, and in Jerusalem, and before his ancients gloriously.

24.19-23 This is possibly referring to the new heaven and the new earth in Rev 21.1. After the tribulation period, and possible nuclear war and destruction, God rebuilds his shattered earth and begins again in righteousness. The high ones, the prince of this world is cast into the bottomless pit for one thousand years. After many days they shall be visited. .after the one thousand years, they are set free to face the great white throne judgment. This is the millennial reign of Jesus Christ, a literal event of one thousand years found in Rev chapter 20. Then Christ shall take to himself his great power, and reign with his people gloriously in the New Jerusalem state.

Chapter 25

25.1-8 O Lord, thou art my God; I will exalt thee, I will praise thy name; for thou hast done wonderful things; thy counsels of old are faithfulness and truth. 2 For thou hast made of a city an heap; of a defenced city a ruin: a palace of strangers to be no city; it shall never be built. 3 Therefore shall the strong people glorify thee, the city of the terrible nations shall fear thee. 4 For thou hast been a strength to the poor, a strength to the needy in his distress, a refuge from the storm, a shadow from the heat, when the blast of the terrible ones is as a storm against the wall. 5 Thou shalt bring down the noise of strangers, as the heat in a dry place; even the heat with the shadow of a cloud: the branch of the terrible ones shall be brought low. 6 And in this mountain shall the Lord of hosts make unto all people a feast of fat things, a feast of wines on the lees, of fat things full of marrow, of wines on the lees well refined. 7 And he will destroy in this mountain the face of the covering cast over all people, and the vail that is spread over all nations. 8 He will swallow up death in victory; and the Lord God will wipe away tears from off all faces; and the rebuke of his people shall he take away from off all the earth: for the Lord hath spoken it.

25.1-8 This chapter opens with a glorious song of victory. It is a spontaneous outburst of unbridled joy. The greatest enemy man has ever faced is conquered. This is the moment God proclaims His victory over death. Death had reigned from Adam, and continued to reign until Christ. At the cross, Jesus Christ took the keys of death out of Satan's hand. In this chapter that event is so dynamic, it causes a spontaneous eruption of joy and song. Christ swallows up death in victory, thus making it disappear. Isaiah sees the marriage supper of the Lamb of Rev 19, possibly as a celebration of the triumph of Jesus Christ over every foe. The world is finally acknowledging the Lordship of Christ, and all creation breaks out in celebration. God has been their refuge from the storm and their shadow from the heat (verse 4).

25.9-12 And it shall be said in that day, Lo, this is our God; we have waited for him, and he will save us: this is the Lord; we have waited for him, we will be glad and rejoice in his salvation. 10 For in this mountain shall the hand of the Lord rest, and Moab shall be trodden down under him, even as straw is trodden down for the dunghill. 11 And he shall spread forth his hands in the midst of them, as he that swimmeth spreadeth forth his hands to swim: and he shall bring down their pride together with the spoils of their hands. 12 And the fortress of the high fort of thy walls shall he bring down, lay low, and bring to the ground, even to the dust.

25.9-12 God is the source of celebration. The salvation of God ignites his people to sing with joy and abandon. Isaiah stands up as choral leader of the church of the future, and praises Jehovah for having destroyed the mighty imperial city, and proved Himself a defense and shield against its tyranny towards His oppressed church. Isaiah stands at the end of time and sings with gusto of God's triumph over every foe. Christ has put every enemy under His feet, including death.

Chapter 26

26.1-4 In that day shall this song be sung in the land of Judah; We have a strong city; salvation will God appoint for walls and bulwarks. 2 Open ye the gates, that the righteous nation which keepeth the truth may enter in. 3 Thou wilt keep him in perfect peace, whose mind is stayed on thee: because he trusteth in thee. 4 Trust ye in the Lord for ever: for in the Lord Jehovah is everlasting strength:

26.1-4 This chapter contains a song of praise for the safety and prosperity of the church, and the destruction of its enemies. The church is represented as a strong city, whose walls and bulwarks are salvation. The gates of salvation are open to all.

26.5-8 For he bringeth down them that dwell on high; the lofty city, he layeth it low; he layeth it low, even to the ground; he bringeth it even to the dust. 6 The foot shall tread it down, even the feet of the poor, and the steps of the needy. 7 The way of the just is uprightness: thou, most upright, dost weigh the path of the just. 8 Yea, in the way of thy judgments, O Lord, have we waited for thee; the desire of our soul is to thy name, and to the remembrance of thee.

26.5-8 God's people have survived every test and trial and now stand victorious with a joyful song of triumph. Evil enemies have been destroyed and trodden under foot. God's righteous judgment has prevailed.

26.9-11 With my soul have I desired thee in the night; yea, with my spirit within me will I seek thee early: for when thy judgments are in the earth, the inhabitants of the world will learn righteousness. 10 Let favour be shewed to the wicked, yet will he not learn righteousness: in the land of uprightness will he deal unjustly, and will not behold the majesty of the Lord. 11 Lord, when thy hand is lifted up, they will not see: but they shall see, and be ashamed for their envy at the people; yea, the fire of thine enemies shall devour them.

26.9-11 With my soul have I desired thee in the night. .The church of the last days, looking back to the past, declares with what longing it has waited for that manifestation of the righteousness of God which has now taken place. Here again the shiir (song), has struck the note of a mâshâl (parable). Proceeding in this tone, the song pauses here once more to reflect: "If favour is shown to the wicked man, he does not learn righteousness."

26.12-19 Lord, thou wilt ordain peace for us: for thou also hast wrought all our works in us. 13 O Lord our God, other lords beside thee have had dominion over us: but by thee only will we make mention of thy name. 14 They are dead, they shall not live; they are deceased, they shall not rise: therefore hast thou visited and destroyed them, and made all their memory to perish. 15 Thou hast increased the nation,

O Lord, thou hast increased the nation: thou art glorified: thou hadst removed it far unto all the ends of the earth. 16 Lord, in trouble have they visited thee, they poured out a prayer when thy chastening was upon them. 17 Like as a woman with child, that draweth near the time of her delivery, is in pain, and crieth out in her pangs; so have we been in thy sight, O Lord. 18 We have been with child, we have been in pain, we have as it were brought forth wind; we have not wrought any deliverance in the earth; neither have the inhabitants of the world fallen. 19 Thy dead men shall live, together with my dead body shall they arise. Awake and sing, ye that dwell in dust: for thy dew is as the dew of herbs, and the earth shall cast out the dead.

26.12-19 The shiir rejoices in the peace of God, so long waited for, has arrived. Jehovah is now King. He seemed indeed to have lost His rule, since the masters of the world had done as they liked with God's people, but it is very different now, and it was only through Jehovah ("through Thee") that the church could now once more gratefully celebrate Jehovah's name. The tyrants who usurped the rule over God's people have now utterly disappeared. "Dead men live not again, shades do not rise again: so hast Thou visited and destroyed them, and caused all their memory to perish."

26.16: Lachash is a quiet, whispering prayer (like the whispering of forms of incantation in Isa 3:3); sorrow renders speechless in the long run; and a consciousness of sin crushes so completely, that a man does not dare to address God aloud (Isa 29:4).

26.19 The tephillah (phylactery) is alluded to. The

phylactery = two black cubes of leather containing parchment inscribed with verses.

26.20-21 Come, my people, enter thou into thy chambers, and shut thy doors about thee: hide thyself as it were for a little moment, until the indignation be overpast. 21 For, behold, the Lord cometh out of his place to punish the inhabitants of the earth for their iniquity: the earth also shall disclose her blood, and shall no more cover her slain.

26.20-21 For, behold, the LORD cometh out of his place to punish the inhabitants. . The prohibition of murder was given to the sons of Noah, and therefore was one of the stipulations of "the covenant of old" (Isa 24:5). The earth supplies two witnesses: (1.) the innocent blood which has been violently shed, which the earth has had to suck up, and which is now exposed, and cries for vengeance; and (2.) the persons themselves who have been murdered in their innocence, and who are slumbering within her. Streams of blood come to light and bear testimony, and martyrs arise to bear witness against their murderers.

Chapter 27

27.1 In that day the Lord with his sore and great and strong sword shall punish leviathan the piercing serpent, even leviathan that crooked serpent; and he shall slay the dragon that is in the sea.

27.1 This chapter refers to the same times as the previous chapters. This is. a new song on the same occasion; it is prophetical of the last times, as the destruction of the anti-Christian powers, and Satan at the head of them. The creatures mentioned represent evil in animal form and refer to Satan and evil world powers. Christ defeats them all. When leviathan shall be destroyed, the vineyard, the Church of God, purged of its blemishes, shall be lovely in God's eyes.

27.2-4 In that day sing ye unto her, A vineyard of red wine. 3 I the Lord do keep it; I will water it every moment: lest any hurt it, I will keep it night and day. 4 Fury is not in me: who would set the briers and thorns against me in battle? I would go through them, I would burn them together.

27.2-4 The vineyard. .the vineyard of 5.1, a vineyard is a spot of ground separated from others, and the church and people of God are separated from the rest of the world by electing, redeeming, and holiness; a vineyard is a place set with various vines, so is the church; there is Christ the true vine, the principal one, which stands in the first place. Jehovah Himself is introduced as speaking. He is the keeper of the vineyard, who waters it every moment when there is any necessity.

27.5 Or let him take hold of my strength, that he may make peace with me; and he shall make peace with me.

27.5 The song closes here. What the church here utters, is the awareness of the gracious protection of her God. Church has assumed her rightful place as the bride of Christ.

27.6-8 He shall cause them that come of Jacob to take root: Israel shall blossom and bud, and fill the face of the world with fruit. 7 Hath he smitten him, as he smote those that smote him? or is he slain according to the slaughter of them that are slain by him? 8 In measure, when it shooteth forth, thou wilt debate with it: he stayeth his rough wind in the day of the east wind.

27.6-8 The prophet here says, in a figure, just the same as the apostle in Rom 11:12, that Israel, when restored once more to favor as a nation, will become "the riches of the Gentiles." it shall be like the mustard tree, when it becomes so great a tree as that the birds of the air make their nests in it; and as the stone cut out of the mountain without hands, when it becomes a great mountain, and fills the whole earth, Mat 13:31.

27.9-11 By this therefore shall the iniquity of Jacob

be purged; and this is all the fruit to take away his sin; when he maketh all the stones of the altar as chalkstones that are beaten in sunder, the groves and images shall not stand up. 10 Yet the defenced city shall be desolate, and the habitation forsaken, and left like a wilderness: there shall the calf feed, and there shall he lie down, and consume the branches thereof. 11 When the boughs thereof are withered, they shall be broken off: the women come, and set them on fire: for it is a people of no understanding: therefore he that made them will not have mercy on them, and he that formed them will shew them no favour.

27.9-11 The groves and the images shall not stand up. . erect, to be worshipped; but shall be thrown down, demolished, and broke to pieces; and, by thus abandoning their idols and idolatrous practices, they will show the sense they have of their sins, and the sincerity of their repentance; and it is to be observed, that the Jews, after their return from the Babylonian captivity, never practiced idolatry again. A curse of 1,000 years was broken.

27.12-13 And it shall come to pass in that day, that the Lord shall beat off from the channel of the river unto the stream of Egypt, and ye shall be gathered one by one, O ye children of Israel. 13 And it shall come to pass in that day, that the great trumpet shall be blown, and they shall come which were ready to perish in the land of Assyria, and the outcasts in the land of Egypt, and shall worship the Lord in the holy mount at Jerusalem.

27.12-13 Repentance changes many things. It changes how God views us, it changes how we view our life, and here it shows how God views His people when they turn to Him again. Then the song of red wine will be sung, (27:2) when God will appear to have taken particular care of his church, and is about to bring it into a flourishing condition; when its troubles and afflictions will come to an end, Jehovah and His people lift their voice in triumphant song. Chapter 27 ends with the greatest choir ever assembled, singing a song of redemption with Christ Himself singing lead.

Chapter 28

28.1 Woe to the crown of pride, to the drunkards of Ephraim, whose glorious beauty is a fading flower, which are on the head of the fat valleys of them that are overcome with wine! 2 Behold, the Lord hath a mighty and strong one, which as a tempest of hail and a destroying storm, as a flood of mighty waters overflowing, shall cast down to the earth with the hand.

28.1-2 This chapter carries us to the earliest years of Hezekiah's reign, probably to the second and third; as Samaria has not yet been destroyed. They run parallel to the book of Micah, which also takes its start from the destruction of Samaria, and are as accurate a mirror of the condition of the people under Hezekiah, as chapters 7-12 were of their condition under Ahaz. In this chapter the ten tribes of Israel and the two tribes of Judah and Benjamin, are threatened with divine judgments, because of their sins and iniquities mentioned. The ten tribes, under the name of Ephraim, for their pride and drunkenness, Isa 28:1. The means of their destruction, the Assyrian monarch, is compared to a hailstorm, and a flood of mighty waters, Isa 28:2. The coming destruction, because of their sins, is repeated, and represented as sudden and swift, when they would be like a fading flower and hasty fruit, Isa 28:4. This theme of judgment upon Ephraim continues until and through chapter 33.

28.3-4 The crown of pride, the drunkards of Ephraim, shall be trodden under feet: 4 And the glorious beauty, which is on the head of the fat valley, shall be a fading flower, and as the hasty fruit before the summer; which when he that looketh upon it seeth, while it is yet in his hand he eateth it up.

28.3-4 Words are scarcely possible with which to express greater sorrow and calamity falling on those who are overcome with wine. God is said to be against them. Their beauty and pride shall fade away. They shall err in judgment, shall have dim vision of truth,. shall lose all sense of moral and religious values, and shall be ensnared with all evil. Their condition shall be heart sickening and hopeless.

28.5-13 In that day shall the Lord of hosts be for a crown of glory, and for a diadem of beauty, unto the residue of his people, 6 And for a spirit of judgment to him that sitteth in judgment, and for strength to them that turn the battle to the gate. 7 But they also have erred through wine, and through strong drink are out of the way; the priest and the prophet have erred through strong drink, they are swallowed up of wine, they are out of the way through strong drink; they err in vision, they stumble in judgment. 8 For all tables are full of vomit and filthiness, so that there is no place clean. 9 Whom shall he teach knowledge? and whom shall he make to understand doctrine? them that are weaned from the milk, and drawn from the breasts. 10 For precept must be upon precept, precept upon precept;

line upon line, line upon line; here a little, and there a little: 11 For with stammering lips and another tongue will he speak to this people. 12 To whom he said, This is the rest wherewith ye may cause the weary to rest; and this is the refreshing: yet they would not hear. 13 But the word of the Lord was unto them precept upon precept, precept upon precept; line upon line, line upon line; here a little, and there a little; that they might go, and fall backward, and be broken, and snared, and taken.

28.5-13 The occasion of this remarkable encounter was probably a feast held to celebrate the renunciation of allegiance to Assyria. What really angered these high and mighty scorners was that the prophet treated them as though they were children only just weaned, and not as masters in Israel. Isaiah gave them the most elementary instruction in the simplest words — words of one syllable, as they put it. They were weary of hearing him repeat the first rudiments of morality, and apply them to the sins and needs of the time. How dare he tutor them who were themselves teachers. How dare he treat them as babes who were grown men, distinguished men, the foremost men and statesmen of the empire. A pretty figure he made too. No one listened to him. It was their advice which was taken, not his, their policy which was followed, not his. And yet he dared come to them, day after day, with the same simple message, the same trite moralities, the same dismal warnings and rebukes. The stammering lips and another tongue no doubt spoke of the coming Assyrians and their lisp in speaking. We see a secondary meaning here that speaks of the coming of the Holy Ghost in Acts chapter two, where God pours out the Holy Ghost with the baptism of other tongues.

28.13 The rest. ."life is one long fatigue. .Christ wants to make it one long rest." They were tired of war, tired of constant threats, tired of judgment, and needed rest. There would be no rest and will never be rest for natural man until he turns to Jesus Christ. Only in Jesus do we find that rest. Jesus proclaims. .come unto me. .and I will give you rest. .Matt 11.28

28.14-15 Wherefore hear the word of the Lord, ye scornful men, that rule this people which is in Jerusalem. 15 Because ye have said, We have made a covenant with death, and with hell are we at agreement; when the overflowing scourge shall pass through, it shall not come unto us: for we have made lies our refuge, and under falsehood have we hid ourselves:

28.14-15 Hear. .ye scornful men. .The prophet replies that when the storm does sweep over the land, as it assuredly will, these "refuges of lies" will prove no shelter to their builders. These false leaders have been tried by the plummet of honesty and righteousness and found to be so out of line that they must come down.

28.16-17 Therefore thus saith the Lord God, Behold, I lay in Zion for a foundation a stone, a tried stone, a precious corner stone, a sure foundation: he that believeth shall not make haste. 17 Judgment also will I lay to the line, and righteousness to the plummet: and the hail shall sweep away the refuge of lies, and the waters shall overflow the hiding place.

28.16-17 A cornerstone. .Jesus Christ is the chief cornerstone; and the man who trusts in that foundation, believing that it really is there, will not be urged to any impatient acts of panic, whatever may be the apparent danger. Both Peter and Paul use this analogy of Christ in the New Testament. Jesus is the corner stone of the sure foundation. Eph 2.20. In the coming storm upon the nation, God has already provided a sure foundation for His people.

28.18-22 And your covenant with death shall be disannulled, and your agreement with hell shall not stand; when the overflowing scourge shall pass through, then ye shall be trodden down by it. 19 From the time that it goeth forth it shall take you: for morning by morning shall it pass over, by day and by night: and it shall be a vexation only to understand the report. 20 For the bed is shorter than that a man can stretch himself on it: and the covering narrower than that he can wrap himself in it. 21 For the Lord shall rise up as in mount Perazim, he shall be wroth as in the valley of Gibeon, that he may do his work, his strange work; and bring to pass his act, his strange act. 22 Now therefore be ye not mockers, lest your bands be made strong: for I have heard from the Lord God of hosts a consumption, even determined upon the whole earth.

28.18-22 And the whip, which Jehovah swings, will not be satisfied with one stroke, but will rain strokes. "And your covenant with death is struck out, and your agreement with Hades will not stand; the swelling scourge, when it comes, ye will become a thing trodden down to it. As often as it passes it takes you: for every morning it passes, by day and by night; and it is nothing but shuddering to hear such preaching. For the bed is too short to stretch in, and the covering too tight when a man wraps himself in it." God had been fighting for Israel, but now He will be fighting against them.

28.23-29 Give ye ear, and hear my voice; hearken, and hear my speech. 24 Doth the plowman plow all day to sow? doth he open and break the clods of his ground? 25 When he hath made plain the face thereof, doth he not cast abroad the fitches, and scatter the cummin, and cast in the principal wheat and the appointed barley and the rie in their place? 26 For his God doth instruct him to discretion, and doth teach him. 27 For the fitches are not threshed with a threshing instrument, neither is a cart wheel turned about upon the cummin; but the fitches are beaten out with a staff, and the cummin with a rod. 28 Bread corn is bruised; because he will not ever be threshing it, nor break it with the wheel of his cart, nor bruise it with his horsemen. 29 This also cometh forth from the Lord of hosts, which is wonderful in counsel, and excellent in working.

28.23-29 The general drift of the parable is obvious. The husbandman does not forever plow or harrow. He ploughs only that he may sow, he harrows the ground only that he may produce a surface on which to plant his seeds. And when he sows, he gives to every seed its appropriate place and use. He scatters the dill and casts the cummin. The wheat he sets, according to the Oriental fashion, in long rows, and the barley in a place specially marked out for it, on the borders of the field, along the edges of the field. And this he does because God has given him discretion. Is God, then, less wise than the farmer He has taught? So, again, when the harvest is gathered in, the wise husbandman still varies and adapts his means to his end. He does not go on threshing forever, his single aim is to separate the chaff from the wheat, to save as much of the grain as he can, and to save it in the best condition he can, that it may be gathered into his garner. He thus varies his modes of treatment, and adapts them to the several kinds of seeds, because God has given him sagacity and wisdom. Will God, then, who gave the husbandman this sagacity, be less observant of time and measure? Will He crush and waste the precious grain of His threshing floor? No. God will save and redeem His chosen people. To the faithful remnant God assures He knows the wheat from the chaff. We are reminded in the New Testament God will separate the chaff from the wheat (Mt 3.12).

Chapter 29

29.1 Woe to Ariel, to Ariel, the city where David dwelt! add ye year to year; let them kill sacrifices.

29.1 Once again the prophet lifts his eyes to view far distant events. He sees the fall of Jerusalem and even further to end time events. His view is so distant he does not see the interim time of the church. This chapter opens the series of prophecies as to the invasion of Judea under Sennacherib, and its deliverance.

29.2 Yet I will distress Ariel, and there shall be heaviness and sorrow: and it shall be unto me as Ariel.

29.2 And there shall be heaviness and sorrow. . .on account of the siege, by reason of the devastations of the enemy without, made on all the cities and towns in Judea round about. This will be because there will be famine and bloodshed in the city.

and it shall be unto me as Ariel. . the whole city shall be as the altar; as that was covered with the blood and carcasses of slain beasts, so this with the blood and carcasses of men

29.3 And I will camp against thee round about, and will lay siege against thee with a mount, and I will raise forts against thee.

29.3 And I will camp against thee. .surely no mortal enemy could attack Jerusalem unless God allowed it to happen. Even then God closely watches and camps round about, to make sure the enemy only goes as far as God permits them to.

29.4 And thou shalt be brought down, and shalt speak out of the ground, and thy speech shall be low out of the dust, and thy voice shall be, as of one that hath a familiar spirit, out of the ground, and thy speech shall whisper out of the dust.

29.4 And thou shalt be brought down to the ground. . warned by Sennacherib's close call, and conquered by Rome.

29.5-8 Moreover the multitude of thy strangers shall be like small dust, and the multitude of the terrible ones shall be as chaff that passeth away: yea, it shall be at an instant suddenly. 6 Thou shalt be visited of the Lord of hosts with thunder, and with earthquake, and great noise, with storm and tempest, and the flame of devouring fire. 7 And the multitude of all the nations that fight against Ariel, even all that fight against her and her munition, and that distress her, shall be as a dream of a night vision. 8 It shall even be as when an hungry man dreameth, and, behold, he eateth; but he awaketh, and his soul is empty: or as when a thirsty man dreameth, and, behold, he drinketh; but he awaketh, and, behold, he is faint, and his soul hath appetite: so shall the

multitude of all the nations be, that fight against mount Zion.

29.5-8 The nations that attack Israel will be many, like small dust, yet will be blown away like chaff. God promises natural intervention to Israel (thunder, earthquakes, noise and storm). The lasting impact of the nations that attack Israel will be like a dream that leaves when awakened. As a man who is hungry and dreams he is eating, then awakes to an empty soul. This is the end result of all nations who gather against Israel.

29.9-12 Stay yourselves, and wonder; cry ye out, and cry: they are drunken, but not with wine; they stagger, but not with strong drink. 10 For the Lord hath poured out upon you the spirit of deep sleep, and hath closed your eyes: the prophets and your rulers, the seers hath he covered. 11 And the vision of all is become unto you as the words of a book that is sealed, which men deliver to one that is learned, saying, Read this, I pray thee: and he saith, I cannot; for it is sealed: 12 And the book is delivered to him that is not learned, saying, Read this, I pray thee: and he saith, I am not learned.

29.9-12 This enigma of the future the prophet holds out before the eyes of his contemporaries. The prophet received it by revelation of Jehovah, and without the illumination of Jehovah it could not possibly be understood. The deep degradation of Jerusalem, the wonderful deliverance, the sudden elevation from the abyss to this lofty height - all this was a matter of faith. But this faith was just what the nation wanted.

29.13-21 Wherefore the Lord said, Forasmuch as this people draw near me with their mouth, and with their

lips do honour me, but have removed their heart far from me, and their fear toward me is taught by the precept of men: 14 Therefore, behold, I will proceed to do a marvellous work among this people, even a marvellous work and a wonder: for the wisdom of their wise men shall perish, and the understanding of their prudent men shall be hid. 15 Woe unto them that seek deep to hide their counsel from the Lord, and their works are in the dark, and they say, Who seeth us? and who knoweth us? 16 Surely your turning of things upside down shall be esteemed as the potter's clay: for shall the work say of him that made it, He made me not? or shall the thing framed say of him that framed it, He had no understanding? 17 Is it not yet a very little while, and Lebanon shall be turned into a fruitful field, and the fruitful field shall be esteemed as a forest? 18 And in that day shall the deaf hear the words of the book, and the eyes of the blind shall see out of obscurity, and out of darkness. 19 The meek also shall increase their joy in the Lord, and the poor among men shall rejoice in the Holy One of Israel. 20 For the terrible one is brought to nought, and the scorner is consumed, and all that watch for iniquity are cut off: 21 That make a man an offender for a word, and lay a snare for him that reproveth in the gate, and turn aside the just for a thing of nought.

29.13-21 This verse (13), is quoted by Jesus as the epitome of what the Pharisees stood for. (Mk7.6-7). The issue is people who draw near with their mouth, but their heart is far from God. He adds their fear of God is taught by men and by precept. True worship must begin in the heart. Because the leaders of the nation would not respond with their hearts, the deaf, blind, meek and poor will replace them. This was a part of the ministry of Jesus, to open blind eyes and deaf ears, both physically and spiritually.

29.22 Therefore thus saith the Lord, who redeemed Abraham, concerning the house of Jacob, Jacob shall not now be ashamed, neither shall his face now wax pale.

29.22 Abraham is mentioned four times in the writing of Isaiah, 29.22, 41.8, 51.2, 63.16.

29.23-24 But when he seeth his children, the work of mine hands, in the midst of him, they shall sanctify my name, and sanctify the Holy One of Jacob, and shall fear the God of Israel. 24 They also that erred in spirit shall come to understanding, and they that murmured shall learn doctrine.

29.23-24 When the descendants of Abraham understand Jesus is their messiah, they will then come to understanding and their blindness will be healed (Rom 11.25)

Chapter 30

30.1-2 Woe to the rebellious children, saith the Lord, that take counsel, but not of me; and that cover with a covering, but not of my spirit, that they may add sin to sin: 2 That walk to go down into Egypt, and have not asked at my mouth; to strengthen themselves in the strength of Pharaoh, and to trust in the shadow of Egypt!

30.1-2 In chapter 30 the negotiations with Egypt are represented as having reached a further stage. An embassy, dispatched for the purpose of concluding a treaty, is already on its way to the court of the Pharaohs. Isaiah takes the position of reiterating God's sense of the frustration of the mission, and derides the folly of those who expect from it any good result. The negotiations by means of ambassadors have already been commenced, but the prophet condemns what he can no longer prevent.

30.3 Therefore shall the strength of Pharaoh be your shame, and the trust in the shadow of Egypt your confusion.

30.3 In essence God says have it your way, you want

Egypt, then Egypt shall be your shame and confusion. This concept of choosing human assistance over God's providence is a continual principal throughout history. From ancient Babylon to the Babylon of the book of Revelation, men fail to seek the true help in God. Why Egypt? The Egyptians had chariots and horses, which the Jews were destitute of. For Palestine, being a country full of steep hills and narrow difficult ways, was in many places impassable by horses, and therefore their beasts of burden were camels, asses, and mules, which are not apt to start, but tread sure in dangerous ways. These beasts of burden served them very well in times of peace. But when they were invaded by armies of the Assyrians and Chaldeans, who had troops of horse, and multitudes of chariots, they wanted the like forces to oppose them; and such the Egyptians could very well supply them with. This is still the concept of many today. God does not get on the level of His adversary. Egypt was on the decline and Assyria. was on the assent, so Israel would be shamed by their alliance.

30.4 For his princes were at Zoan, and his ambassadors came to Hanes.

30.4 Zoan was the largest city of Egypt near the border. Apparently some were wanting to flee for safety to this Egyptian city and Isaiah is telling them the folly of this decision. God had delivered their forefathers from Egypt, now they were going back.

30.5-7 They were all ashamed of a people that could not profit them, nor be an help nor profit, but a shame, and also a reproach. 6 The burden of the beasts of the south: into the land of trouble and anguish, from whence come the young and old lion, the viper and

fiery flying serpent, they will carry their riches upon the shoulders of young asses, and their treasures upon the bunches of camels, to a people that shall not profit them. 7 For the Egyptians shall help in vain, and to no purpose: therefore have I cried concerning this, Their strength is to sit still.

30.5-7 Hezekiah would send gifts to Egypt on beasts of burden. these beasts would be attacked by the animals of prey, (vipers and fiery serpents), on the journey. The journey would be hard on the beasts, but most of all Egypt would accept Hezekiah's gifts and be of no value, as the nation no longer could defend against its enemies.

30.8-17 Now go, write it before them in a table, and note it in a book, that it may be for the time to come for ever and ever: 9 That this is a rebellious people, lying children, children that will not hear the law of the Lord: 10 Which say to the seers, See not; and to the prophets, Prophesy not unto us right things, speak unto us smooth things, prophesy deceits: 11 Get you out of the way, turn aside out of the path, cause the Holy One of Israel to cease from before us. 12 Wherefore thus saith the Holy One of Israel, Because ye despise this word, and trust in oppression and perverseness, and stay thereon: 13 Therefore this iniquity shall be to you as a breach ready to fall, swelling out in a high wall, whose breaking cometh suddenly at an instant. 14 And he shall break it as the breaking of the potters' vessel that is broken in pieces; he shall not spare: so that there shall not be found in the bursting of it a sherd to take fire from the hearth, or to take water withal out of the pit. 15 For thus saith the Lord God, the Holy One of Israel; In returning and rest shall ye be saved; in quietness and in confidence shall be your strength: and ye would not. 16 But ye said, No; for we will flee upon horses; therefore shall ye flee: and, We will ride upon the swift; therefore shall they that pursue you be swift. 17 One thousand shall flee at the rebuke of one; at the rebuke of five shall ye flee: till ye be left as a beacon upon the top of a mountain, and as an ensign on an hill.

30.8-17 God instructs Isaiah to write the prophesies in a book for future generations. The reason for this is of course God's alone, but we can speculate maybe because the people were not giving a genuine heart felt response?. The people were described as a rebellious people (9). They had refused truth and wanted smooth things said. They preferred deceit to truth. While they sought peace with the nations around them, they failed to seek peace with Almighty God. Their only hope lay in returning and rest, this would be their salvation. They refuse and seek to escape.

30.18-26 And therefore will the Lord wait, that he may be gracious unto you, and therefore will he be exalted, that he may have mercy upon you: for the Lord is a God of judgment: blessed are all they that wait for him. 19 For the people shall dwell in Zion at Jerusalem: thou shalt weep no more: he will be very gracious unto thee at the voice of thy cry; when he shall hear it, he will answer thee. 20 And though the Lord give you the bread of adversity, and the water of affliction, yet shall not thy teachers be removed into a corner any more, but thine eyes shall see thy teachers: 21 And thine ears shall hear a word behind thee, saying, This is the way, walk ye in it, when ye turn to the right hand, and when ye turn to the left. 22 Ye shall defile

also the covering of thy graven images of silver, and the ornament of thy molten images of gold: thou shalt cast them away as a menstruous cloth; thou shalt say unto it, Get thee hence. 23 Then shall he give the rain of thy seed, that thou shalt sow the ground withal; and bread of the increase of the earth, and it shall be fat and plenteous: in that day shall thy cattle feed in large pastures. 24 The oxen likewise and the young asses that ear the ground shall eat clean provender, which hath been winnowed with the shovel and with the fan. 25 And there shall be upon every high mountain, and upon every high hill, rivers and streams of waters in the day of the great slaughter, when the towers fall. 26 Moreover the light of the moon shall be as the light of the sun, and the light of the sun shall be sevenfold, as the light of seven days, in the day that the Lord bindeth up the breach of his people, and healeth the stroke of their wound.

30.18-26 Therefore will the Lord wait. . the value of waiting is here taught by God himself. He waits. Waiting teaches so many things. God always blesses those who wait on Him. Even though adversity, and without teachers to instruct, God says there is always a voice saying this is the way, walk in it. This passage became an encouragement to the New Testament church, as it became known as "The Way." The process of waiting purifies us and then opens the windows of blessing to be poured out in our lives. After the bread of affliction and water of adversity, there is abundance and fullness to those who wait on God.

30.27-33 Behold, the name of the Lord cometh from far, burning with his anger, and the burden thereof is heavy: his lips are full of indignation, and his tongue as a devouring fire: **28 And his breath, as an overflowing stream, shall reach to the midst of the neck, to sift the nations with the sieve of vanity: and there shall be a bridle in the jaws of the people, causing them to err. 29 Ye shall have a song, as in the night when a holy solemnity is kept; and gladness of heart, as when one goeth with a pipe to come into the mountain of the Lord, to the mighty One of Israel. 30 And the Lord shall cause his glorious voice to be heard, and shall shew the lighting down of his arm, with the indignation of his anger, and with the flame of a devouring fire, with scattering, and tempest, and hailstones. 31 For through the voice of the Lord shall the Assyrian be beaten down, which smote with a rod. 32 And in every place where the grounded staff shall pass, which the Lord shall lay upon him, it shall be with tabrets and harps: and in battles of shaking will he fight with it. 33 For Tophet is ordained of old; yea, for the king it is prepared; he hath made it deep and large: the pile thereof is fire and much wood; the breath of the Lord, like a stream of brimstone, doth kindle it.**

30.27-33 The contrast is stark. On one hand blessing and comfort to those who have waited patiently on God. The other side is burning and anger and fear to those who reject God. While mayhem reigns all around, God's true people have a song in the night, with gladness of heart. God's glorious voice is heard and the stereo effect is joy and gladness to one and fear and judgment to the other. Thus will it always and ever be. Tophet, the valley of burning, waits for those deaf to God's appeal. The very breath of God ignites the valley of eternal fire.

Chapter 31

31.1-4 Woe to them that go down to Egypt for help; and stay on horses, and trust in chariots, because they are many; and in horsemen, because they are very strong; but they look not unto the Holy One of Israel, neither seek the Lord! 2 Yet he also is wise, and will bring evil, and will not call back his words: but will arise against the house of the evildoers, and against the help of them that work iniquity. 3 Now the Egyptians are men, and not God; and their horses flesh, and not spirit. When the Lord shall stretch out his hand, both he that helpeth shall fall, and he that is holpen shall fall down, and they all shall fail together. 4 For thus hath the Lord spoken unto me, Like as the lion and the young lion roaring on his prey, when a multitude of shepherds is called forth against him, he will not be afraid of their voice, nor abase himself for the noise of them: so shall the Lord of hosts come down to fight for mount Zion, and for the hill thereof.

31.1-4. The theme continues, to trust in man is a tragic choice. Horses and chariots are a poor substitute for God's provision and protection. (3) For the Egyptians are men and not God. Isaiah is continuing to lift his voice against those who trust in Egypt.

31.5-9 As birds flying, so will the Lord of hosts defend Jerusalem; defending also he will deliver it; and passing over he will preserve it. 6 Turn ye unto him from whom the children of Israel have deeply revolted. 7 For in that day every man shall cast away his idols of silver, and his idols of gold, which your own hands have made unto you for a sin. 8 Then shall the Assyrian fall with the sword, not of a mighty man; and the sword, not of a mean man, shall devour him: but he shall flee from the sword, and his young men shall be discomfited. 9 And he shall pass over to his strong hold for fear, and his princes shall be afraid of the ensign, saith the Lord, whose fire is in Zion, and his furnace in Jerusalem.

31.5-9 The destruction of Assyria is again forecast. Surely this is a voice of welcome to the hurting populace of the faithful remnant. Assyria is depicted as a winged Lion, and God pointedly states this lion shall be repulsed. Isaiah is warning King Hezekiah again that the law of God in Deut 17.16 forbade them to trust in horses and in Egypt. So full were Egyptian politics of bluster and big language, that the Hebrews had a nickname for Egypt. They called her Rahab, which means "Stormy speech," "Blusterer," "Braggart." It was the term also for the crocodile, as being a monster, so that there was a mocking as well as moral aptness in the name. Isaiah, catching at the old name, and putting to it another use which describes Egyptian uselessness,. calls her "Rahab sit-still," "Braggart-that-sitteth-still," "Stormy-speech stay-at-home." Isaiah mocks Egypt as Rahab. He is saying Egypt is all talk, a loud mouth that never comes through with her promises of help. This proved true as all prophecy from God does.

Chapter 32

32.1-8 Behold, a king shall reign in righteousness, and princes shall rule in judgment. 2 And a man shall be as an hiding place from the wind, and a covert from the tempest; as rivers of water in a dry place, as the shadow of a great rock in a weary land. 3 And the eyes of them that see shall not be dim, and the ears of them that hear shall hearken. 4 The heart also of the rash shall understand knowledge, and the tongue of the stammerers shall be ready to speak plainly. 5 The vile person shall be no more called liberal, nor the churl said to be bountiful. 6 For the vile person will speak villany, and his heart will work iniquity, to practice hypocrisy, and to utter error against the Lord, to make empty the soul of the hungry, and he will cause the drink of the thirsty to fail. 7 The instruments also of the churl are evil: he deviseth wicked devices to destroy the poor with lying words, even when the needy speaketh right. 8 But the liberal deviseth liberal things; and by liberal things shall he stand.

32.1-8 Again Isaiah takes writing instrument in hand to assure the nation that God will eventually take His rightful place as the King of Kings in a future reign on this earth. This should comfort the people in times of national crises. Jesus Christ is the man who is the hiding place and the covert from the storm. The opening of eyes and ears began in the earthly ministry of Jesus.

32.9-15 Rise up, ye women that are at ease; hear my voice, ye careless daughters; give ear unto my speech. 10 Many days and years shall ye be troubled, ye careless women: for the vintage shall fail, the gathering shall not come. 11 Tremble, ye women that are at ease; be troubled, ye careless ones: strip you, and make you bare, and gird sackcloth upon your loins. 12 They shall lament for the teats, for the pleasant fields, for the fruitful vine. 13 Upon the land of my people shall come up thorns and briers; yea, upon all the houses of joy in the joyous city: 14 Because the palaces shall be forsaken; the multitude of the city shall be left; the forts and towers shall be for dens for ever, a joy of wild asses, a pasture of flocks; 15 Until the spirit be poured upon us from on high, and the wilderness be a fruitful field, and the fruitful field be counted for a forest.

32.9-15 Warning the women to not be careless. Possibly this refers to the upper class women who were wealthy. Amos also speaks this in Amos 4.1. There seems to be a consensus among the prophets that women were particularly carnal at this time in Judah.

32.16-20 Then judgment shall dwell in the wilderness, and righteousness remain in the fruitful field. 17 And the work of righteousness shall be peace; and the effect of righteousness quietness and assurance for ever. 18 And my people shall dwell in a peaceable habitation, and in sure dwellings, and in quiet resting places; 19 When it shall hail, coming down on the forest; and the

city shall be low in a low place. 20 Blessed are ye that sow beside all waters, that send forth thither the feet of the ox and the ass.

32.16-20 This theme is also voiced by Amos in 5.24. This was made famous in Martin Luther King Jr's famous speech "I have a dream." God's people will one day dwell in a peaceable habitation. . . . .

Chapter 33

33.1-4 Woe to thee that spoilest, and thou wast not spoiled; and dealest treacherously, and they dealt not treacherously with thee! when thou shalt cease to spoil, thou shalt be spoiled; and when thou shalt make an end to deal treacherously, they shall deal treacherously with thee. 2 O Lord, be gracious unto us; we have waited for thee: be thou their arm every morning, our salvation also in the time of trouble. 3 At the noise of the tumult the people fled; at the lifting up of thyself the nations were scattered. 4 And your spoil shall be gathered like the gathering of the caterpiller: as the running to and fro of locusts shall he run upon them.

33.1-4. We are now in the fourteenth year of Hezekiah's reign. The threatenings of the first years, which the repentance of the people had delayed, are now in force again, and actually realized. The Assyrians are already in Judah, and have not only devastated the land, but are threatening Jerusalem. The element of promise now gains the upper hand, the prophet places himself between Assyria and his own nation with the weapons of prophecy and prayer. While the prophet is praying thus, he already sees the answer. The people are fleeing and the spoil is gathered from mighty Assyria.

33.5-6 The Lord is exalted; for he dwelleth on high: he hath filled Zion with judgment and righteousness. 6 And wisdom and knowledge shall be the stability of thy times, and strength of salvation: the fear of the Lord is his treasure.

33.5-6 Isaiah sees the results of the victory God gives: wisdom, knowledge and strength of salvation.

33.7-10 Behold, their valiant ones shall cry without: the ambassadors of peace shall weep bitterly. 8 The highways lie waste, the wayfaring man ceaseth: he hath broken the covenant, he hath despised the cities, he regardeth no man. 9 The earth mourneth and languisheth: Lebanon is ashamed and hewn down: Sharon is like a wilderness; and Bashan and Carmel shake off their fruits. 10 Now will I rise, saith the Lord; now will I be exalted; now will I lift up myself.

33.7-10 The valiant ones or ambassadors listed by the prophet were the messengers sent to Sennacherib to seek for peace. They carried to him the amount of silver and gold, which he had demanded as the condition of peace (2Ki 18:14). But Sennacherib broke the treaty, by demanding nothing less than the surrender of Jerusalem itself. Then the ambassadors of Jerusalem cried aloud, when they arrived at Jerusalem, and had to convey this message of disgrace and alarm to the king and nation. They weep bitterly over such a breach of faith, deception and disgrace.

33.11 Ye shall conceive chaff, ye shall bring forth stubble: your breath, as fire, shall devour you.

33.11 Isaiah informs Assyria that the fire of their own wrath will turn and consume them.

33.12 And the people shall be as the burnings of lime: as thorns cut up shall they be burned in the fire.

33.12 Burning of lime signifies complete destruction, only ashes left, and thorns, signifies the quickness of the burning.

33.13-14 Hear, ye that are far off, what I have done; and, ye that are near, acknowledge my might. 14 The sinners in Zion are afraid; fearfulness hath surprised the hypocrites. Who among us shall dwell with the devouring fire? who among us shall dwell with everlasting burnings?

33.13-14 In these two verses Isaiah again remonstrates Judah to be aware of the force of God's anger on those far away as well as the people of Judah.

33.15-17 He that walketh righteously, and speaketh uprightly; he that despiseth the gain of oppressions, that shaketh his hands from holding of bribes, that stoppeth his ears from hearing of blood, and shutteth his eyes from seeing evil; 16 He shall dwell on high: his place of defence shall be the munitions of rocks: bread shall be given him; his waters shall be sure. 17 Thine eyes shall see the king in his beauty: they shall behold the land that is very far off.

33.15-17 God is always just. He assures those that walk

in righteousness shall be rewarded. The judgment all around them will not cause God to lose sight of righteous people. They shall see the King in His beauty.

33.18-24 Thine heart shall meditate terror. Where is the scribe? where is the receiver? where is he that counted the towers? 19 Thou shalt not see a fierce people, a people of a deeper speech than thou canst perceive; of a stammering tongue, that thou canst not understand. 20 Look upon Zion, the city of our solemnities: thine eyes shall see Jerusalem a quiet habitation, a tabernacle that shall not be taken down; not one of the stakes thereof shall ever be removed, neither shall any of the cords thereof be broken. 21 But there the glorious Lord will be unto us a place of broad rivers and streams; wherein shall go no galley with oars, neither shall gallant ship pass thereby. 22 For the Lord is our judge, the Lord is our lawgiver, the Lord is our king; he will save us. 23 Thy tacklings are loosed; they could not well strengthen their mast, they could not spread the sail: then is the prey of a great spoil divided; the lame take the prey. 24 And the inhabitant shall not say, I am sick: the people that dwell therein shall be forgiven their iniquity.

33.18-24 Even though the hearts meditated terror, Jerusalem stands there unconquered and inviolable, the fortress where the congregation of the whole land celebrates its feasts. It is a city of quiet habitation with a tabernacle to receive their sacrifices. Their link to God is yet intact and is not swept away in the bitter fires of judgment. God will yet be victorious and be a place of broad rivers and streams. One great peculiarity of Jerusalem, which distinguishes it from almost all other historical cities, is that it has no river. Babylon was on the Euphrates, Nineveh on the Tigris, Thebes on the Nile, Rome on the Tiber; but Jerusalem had nothing but a fountain or two, and a well or two, and a little trickle of an intermittent stream. God is to be the supply of Jerusalem. He is their river. Places near broad rivers produce a great variety of plants. The children of Israel regretted that they had left the leeks, and garlic, and onions, and cucumbers, and melons of Egypt, plants that grew by the rivers. Where there are rivers there is an abundance of fish of all kinds, and in the fat pastures, such as Goshen, which was well watered by the Nile, abundance of cattle are reared. God is all this and more to His Church. God, the judge, the lawgiver, the King, will save his people. Isaiah again demonstrates why he is the Shakespeare of Hebrew literature. These poetic lines reverberate with hope and confidence in God.

Chapter 34

34.1 Come near, ye nations, to hear; and hearken, ye people: let the earth hear, and all that is therein; the world, and all things that come forth of it.

34.1 Armageddon, the very word conjures horrible fear and panic. In this chapter Isaiah unveils the future horror of this incredible battle. This chapter spells out that final chapter on the judgment of the world. It is fairly certain Jeremiah had this chapter and chapter 35 before him when he wrote many of his prophecies. (Jeremiah chapters 25, 46, 50,51). This chapter draws back the curtain, which separates the visible world from the invisible. It reveals celestial regions, in which there are also great struggles going on. It lifts up our eyes to the grander movements of the world of spirits; and then it declares that the sword which is to be used in fighting.

34.2 For the indignation of the Lord is upon all nations, and his fury upon all their armies: he hath utterly destroyed them, he hath delivered them to the slaughter.

34.2 All nations. . these are the nations which have

committed fornication with the scarlet woman of Rev 18.3 in false worship and idolatry.

34.3-4 Their slain also shall be cast out, and their stink shall come up out of their carcases, and the mountains shall be melted with their blood. 4 And all the host of heaven shall be dissolved, and the heavens shall be rolled together as a scroll: and all their host shall fall down, as the leaf falleth off from the vine, and as a falling fig from the fig tree. . . . .
. . . .
. . . .
. . . .

34.3-4 This chapter draws back the curtain, which separates the visible world from the invisible. It reveals celestial regions, in which there are also great struggles going on. It lifts up our eyes to the world of spirits; and then it declares that the sword, which is to be used in fighting what seem to be the petty wars of the Hebrews and the Edomites, is the same sword, which has been used, in these celestial conflicts. The means of righteousness upon the earth must be the same as the means of righteousness in the heavens.

34.5-6 For my sword shall be bathed in heaven: behold, it shall come down upon Idumea, and upon the people of my curse, to judgment. 6 The sword of the Lord is filled with blood, it is made fat with fatness, and with the blood of lambs and goats, with the fat of the kidneys of rams: for the Lord hath a sacrifice in Bozrah, and a great slaughter in the land of Idumea.

34.5-6 In ancient times soldiers bathed their swords in various things to harden them in battle. God's sword is bathed in blood of the many sacrifices Israel offered in insincerity.

34.7-15 And the unicorns shall come down with them, and the bullocks with the bulls; and their land shall be soaked with blood, and their dust made fat with fatness. 8 For it is the day of the Lord's vengeance, and the year of recompences for the controversy of Zion. 9 And the streams thereof shall be turned into pitch, and the dust thereof into brimstone, and the land thereof shall become burning pitch. 10 It shall not be quenched night nor day; the smoke thereof shall go up for ever: from generation to generation it shall lie waste; none shall pass through it for ever and ever. 11 But the cormorant and the bittern shall possess it; the owl also and the raven shall dwell in it: and he shall stretch out upon it the line of confusion, and the stones of emptiness. 12 They shall call the nobles thereof to the kingdom, but none shall be there, and all her princes shall be nothing. 13 And thorns shall come up in her palaces, nettles and brambles in the fortresses thereof: and it shall be an habitation of dragons, and a court for owls. 14 The wild beasts of the desert shall also meet with the wild beasts of the island, and the satyr shall cry to his fellow; the screech owl also shall rest there, and find for herself a place of rest. 15 There shall the great owl make her nest, and lay, and hatch, and gather under her shadow: there shall the vultures also be gathered, every one with her mate.

34.7-15 This chapter is against Edom the other twin against which Jacob was prophesied. Edom here represents all mankind who live after the flesh and the sensual. The contrast will be complete in Chapter 35 when the prophet contrasts the end of the righteous with that of Edom in this chapter. Edom shall become the habitation of evil animals and desolate.

34.16-17 Seek ye out of the book of the Lord, and read: no one of these shall fail, none shall want her mate: for my mouth it hath commanded, and his spirit it hath gathered them. 17 And he hath cast the lot for them, and his hand hath divided it unto them by line: they shall possess it for ever, from generation to generation shall they dwell therein.

34.16-17 The prophet encourages the people to seek out the scriptures to see for themselves that this is prophesied to come to pass. This passage is used even today to seek not only the scriptures, but the mate to each scripture, to establish its sure meaning. No scripture shall want for its fulfillment, all shall come to pass. The bible is a book given by God and is perfect in its compilation.

Chapter 35

35.1-2 The wilderness and the solitary place shall be glad for them; and the desert shall rejoice, and blossom as the rose. 2 It shall blossom abundantly, and rejoice even with joy and singing: the glory of Lebanon shall be given unto it, the excellency of Carmel and Sharon, they shall see the glory of the Lord, and the excellency of our God.

35.1-2 Now the contrast to the barrenness of the previous chapter. The wilderness and desert of God's true people will blossom as the rose. It will blossom with singing and rejoicing. Possibly this also means a moral wilderness that blossoms when Jesus Christ comes to the earth.

35.3-7 Strengthen ye the weak hands, and confirm the feeble knees. 4 Say to them that are of a fearful heart, Be strong, fear not: behold, your God will come with vengeance, even God with a recompence; he will come and save you. 5 Then the eyes of the blind shall be opened, and the ears of the deaf shall be unstopped. 6 Then shall the lame man leap as an hart, and the tongue of the dumb sing: for in the wilderness shall waters break out, and streams in the desert. 7 And the

parched ground shall become a pool, and the thirsty land springs of water: in the habitation of dragons, where each lay, shall be grass with reeds and rushes.

35.3-7 This is the passage Jesus used of himself when His cousin John the Baptist was confined to prison and sent disciples to Jesus to ask if Jesus was truly the messiah, or should he look for another. (Matt 11.3) Jesus told John's disciples to tell. John what they saw and heard. When John's disciples reported blind eyes were opened, the dumb spoke, and the lame walked, then John the Baptist knew their God had come in the flesh. The barren 400 years of silence and dryness had ended and moral and spiritual streams were flowing. The empty parched hearts of mankind were to be filled with waters. In John 7.37 Jesus himself speaks of this when He tells them out of their bellies shall flow rivers of living water. This is a direct prophecy of the outpouring of the Holy Ghost in Acts chapter two.

35.8-10 And an highway shall be there, and a way, and it shall be called The way of holiness; the unclean shall not pass over it; but it shall be for those: the wayfaring men, though fools, shall not err therein. 9 No lion shall be there, nor any ravenous beast shall go up thereon, it shall not be found there; but the redeemed shall walk there: 10 And the ransomed of the Lord shall return, and come to Zion with songs and everlasting joy upon their heads: they shall obtain joy and gladness, and sorrow and sighing shall flee away.

35.8-10 God will provide a way. In fact it will be a highway in the wilderness. It will be a way of holiness. We are instructed in Heb 12.14 without holiness no man shall see the Lord. To walk on this highway God informs the traveller they must be holy. The benefits of this highway are many. There shall be no predators on this highway. It shall only be travelled by the redeemed. It is populated with people on their way to Zion. This throng of multitudes down through the ages has obtained joy and gladness, and continually break forth into songs that speak of everlasting joy. For the first time in man's recorded history, sorrow and sighing flees away.

Chapter 36

36.1 Now it came to pass in the fourteenth year of king Hezekiah, that Sennacherib king of Assyria came up against all the defenced cities of Judah, and took them.

36.1 These two chapters relate the incredible events of the deliverance of Jerusalem form the Assyrian challenge. Sennacherib was one of the most magnificent of the Assyrian kings.
He seems to have been the first who fixed the seat of government permanently at Nineveh, which he carefully repaired and adorned with splendid buildings. His greatest work is the grand palace at Koyunjik, which covered a space of about eight acres, and was adorned throughout with sculptures.

36.2 And the king of Assyria sent Rabshakeh from Lachish to Jerusalem unto king Hezekiah with a great army. And he stood by the conduit of the upper pool in the highway of the fuller's field.

36.2 This general was probably on his way to Egypt and was planning to conquer Jerusalem on his way. Little did he know his whole life would change when he encountered the people of promise.

Rabshakeh~Rabshakeh or Rab-Sak, the chief cupbearer, or general staff-officer in the Assyrian service, entrusted with diplomatic business. It is the title of an office, and not the name of a person.

36.3-22 Then came forth unto him Eliakim, Hilkiah's son, which was over the house, and Shebna the scribe, and Joah, Asaph's son, the recorder. 4 And Rabshakeh said unto them, Say ye now to Hezekiah, Thus saith the great king, the king of Assyria, What confidence is this wherein thou trustest? 5 I say, sayest thou, (but they are but vain words) I have counsel and strength for war: now on whom dost thou trust, that thou rebellest against me? 6 Lo, thou trustest in the staff of this broken reed, on Egypt; whereon if a man lean, it will go into his hand, and pierce it: so is Pharaoh king of Egypt to all that trust in him. 7 But if thou say to me, We trust in the Lord our God: is it not he, whose high places and whose altars Hezekiah hath taken away, and said to Judah and to Jerusalem, Ye shall worship before this altar? 8 Now therefore give pledges, I pray thee, to my master the king of Assyria, and I will give thee two thousand horses, if thou be able on thy part to set riders upon them. 9 How then wilt thou turn away the face of one captain of the least of my master's servants, and put thy trust on Egypt for chariots and for horsemen? 10 And am I now come up without the Lord against this land to destroy it? the Lord said unto me, Go up against this land, and destroy it. 11 Then said Eliakim and Shebna and Joah unto Rabshakeh, Speak, I pray thee, unto thy servants in the Syrian language; for we understand it: and speak not to us in the Jews' language, in the ears of the people that are on the wall. 12 But Rabshakeh said, Hath my master sent me to thy master and to

thee to speak these words? hath he not sent me to the men that sit upon the wall, that they may eat their own dung, and drink their own piss with you? 13 Then Rabshakeh stood, and cried with a loud voice in the Jews' language, and said, Hear ye the words of the great king, the king of Assyria. 14 Thus saith the king, Let not Hezekiah deceive you: for he shall not be able to deliver you. 15 Neither let Hezekiah make you trust in the Lord, saying, The Lord will surely deliver us: this city shall not be delivered into the hand of the king of Assyria. 16 Hearken not to Hezekiah: for thus saith the king of Assyria, Make an agreement with me by a present, and come out to me: and eat ye every one of his vine, and every one of his fig tree, and drink ye every one the waters of his own cistern; 17 Until I come and take you away to a land like your own land, a land of corn and wine, a land of bread and vineyards. 18 Beware lest Hezekiah persuade you, saying, the Lord will deliver us. Hath any of the gods of the nations delivered his land out of the hand of the king of Assyria? 19 Where are the gods of Hamath and Arphad? where are the gods of Sepharvaim? and have they delivered Samaria out of my hand? 20 Who are they among all the gods of these lands, that have delivered their land out of my hand, that the Lord should deliver Jerusalem out of my hand? 21 But they held their peace, and answered him not a word: for the king's commandment was, saying, Answer him not. 22 Then came Eliakim, the son of Hilkiah, that was over the household, and Shebna the scribe, and Joah, the son of Asaph, the recorder, to Hezekiah with their clothes rent, and told him the words of Rabshakeh.

36.3-22 This is the confrontation between the spokesman of the Assyrian army and the officers of King Hezekiah.

This is the historical climax of the people of God turning to Egypt for help in place of God. God will prove conclusively to his people they should depend on Him and not on the arm of flesh. Egypt cannot save them, but God miraculously saves them. The captain of the army of Assyria mocks them, and challenges them to resist. Ultimately, Isaiah tells Hezekiah. that God will see the nation through. The enemy specifically tells the Hebrew people not to believe in Hezekiah. Rabshakeh boasts of the many countries that have been conquered. Hezekiah's emissaries answer not a word as they are commanded to remain silent. As this chapter closes, it looks hopeless for Jerusalem. The stage is set for one of the most dramatic victories for the nation of Israel.

Chapter 37

37.1-5 And it came to pass, when king Hezekiah heard it, that he rent his clothes, and covered himself with sackcloth, and went into the house of the Lord. 2 And he sent Eliakim, who was over the household, and Shebna the scribe, and the elders of the priests covered with sackcloth, unto Isaiah the prophet the son of Amoz. 3 And they said unto him, Thus saith Hezekiah, This day is a day of trouble, and of rebuke, and of blasphemy: for the children are come to the birth, and there is not strength to bring forth. 4 It may be the Lord thy God will hear the words of Rabshakeh, whom the king of Assyria his master hath sent to reproach the living God, and will reprove the words which the Lord thy God hath heard: wherefore lift up thy prayer for the remnant that is left. 5 So the servants of king Hezekiah came to Isaiah.

37.1-5 This chapter would certainly record one of the highest moments of Isaiah's prophetical career. He stood alone in the tempest in his absolute faith in God. In this chapter the Assyrian army surrounds Jerusalem. The emissaries of Assyria have made their boast and have ample evidence of other conquered cities to back up their threat. When King Hezekiah hears it he is beside himself with fear. He rents his clothes, a sign of terror or extreme distress. He goes to the temple and sends for Isaiah. Their doubt and fear are palpable.

37.6-8 And Isaiah said unto them, Thus shall ye say unto your master, Thus saith the Lord, Be not afraid of the words that thou hast heard, wherewith the servants of the king of Assyria have blasphemed me. 7 Behold, I will send a blast upon him, and he shall hear a rumour, and return to his own land; and I will cause him to fall by the sword in his own land. 8 So Rabshakeh returned, and found the king of Assyria warring against Libnah: for he had heard that he was departed from Lachish.

37.6-8 Isaiah is as confident as they are distressed. Isaiah calmly assures them God will send a blast on the Assyrian army, he will hear a rumor and return home. So Rabshakeh returns to his own land.

37.9-13 And he heard say concerning Tirhakah king of Ethiopia, He is come forth to make war with thee. And when he heard it, he sent messengers to Hezekiah, saying, 10 Thus shall ye speak to Hezekiah king of Judah, saying, Let not thy God, in whom thou trustest, deceive thee, saying, Jerusalem shall not be given into the hand of the king of Assyria. 11 Behold, thou hast heard what the kings of Assyria have done to all lands by destroying them utterly; and shalt thou be delivered? 12 Have the gods of the nations delivered them which my fathers have destroyed, as Gozan, and Haran, and Rezeph, and the children of Eden which were in Telassar? 13 Where is the king of Hamath, and the king of Arphad, and the king of the city of Sepharvaim, Hena, and Ivah?

37.9-13 Now Isaiah hears news of the other approach of the Egyptians from the other direction. Judah is a small nation on the chessboard of world powers. Isaiah hears this somber news and sends word to the King assuring him Jerusalem is safe, and Jerusalem will not be given to Assyria. The conquest of other nations held up as proof Judah will also fall to the Assyrians, is dismissed by Isaiah. This is The King of Kings the Assyrians now challenge. This outcome will indeed be radically different than other nations. God is again about to reveal to the world the Jewish people are his signal treasure in the earth.

37.14-20 And Hezekiah received the letter from the hand of the messengers, and read it: and Hezekiah went up unto the house of the Lord, and spread it before the Lord. 15 And Hezekiah prayed unto the Lord, saying, 16 O Lord of hosts, God of Israel, that dwellest between the cherubims, thou art the God, even thou alone, of all the kingdoms of the earth: thou hast made heaven and earth. 17 Incline thine ear, O Lord, and hear; open thine eyes, O Lord, and see: and hear all the words of Sennacherib, which hath sent to reproach the living God. 18 Of a truth, Lord, the kings of Assyria have laid waste all the nations, and their countries, 19 And have cast their gods into the fire: for they were no gods, but the work of men's hands, wood and stone: therefore they have destroyed them. 20 Now therefore, O Lord our God, save us from his hand, that all the kingdoms of the earth may know that thou art the Lord, even thou only.

37.14-20 Hezekiah takes the letter of threat to the Lord and puts it on the altar, and prays. Hezekiah has reached the end of human help and so turns to his God. This is the moment God has been patiently waiting for. God longs to be the true King of Judah, and God steps up to prove his Kingship.

37.21-29 Then Isaiah the son of Amoz sent unto Hezekiah, saying, Thus saith the Lord God of Israel, Whereas thou hast prayed to me against Sennacherib king of Assyria: 22 This is the word which the Lord hath spoken concerning him; The virgin, the daughter of Zion, hath despised thee, and laughed thee to scorn; the daughter of Jerusalem hath shaken her head at thee. 23 Whom hast thou reproached and blasphemed? and against whom hast thou exalted thy voice, and lifted up thine eyes on high? even against the Holy One of Israel. 24 By thy servants hast thou reproached the Lord, and hast said, By the multitude of my chariots am I come up to the height of the mountains, to the sides of Lebanon; and I will cut down the tall cedars thereof, and the choice fir trees thereof: and I will enter into the height of his border, and the forest of his Carmel. 25 I have digged, and drunk water; and with the sole of my feet have I dried up all the rivers of the besieged places. 26 Hast thou not heard long ago, how I have done it; and of ancient times, that I have formed it? now have I brought it to pass, that thou shouldest be to lay waste defenced cities into ruinous heaps. 27 Therefore their inhabitants were of small power, they were dismayed and confounded: they were as the grass of the field, and as the green herb, as the grass on the housetops, and as corn blasted before it be grown up. 28 But I know thy abode, and thy going out, and thy coming in, and thy rage against me. 29 Because thy rage against me, and thy tumult, is come up into mine ears, therefore will I put my hook in

thy nose, and my bridle in thy lips, and I will turn thee back by the way by which thou camest.

37.21-29 God always uses men. God will not work without a man. God speaks to Isaiah to relay His message to the King Hezekiah. Interesting that the Assyrians were challenging Jerusalem, but from God's point of view, they challenged God himself. Can you imagine how God must have laughed when the Syrian boasted how many chariots they had? (24). The Assyrian prattles on and on of his prowess and might.

37.30-35 And this shall be a sign unto thee, Ye shall eat this year such as groweth of itself; and the second year that which springeth of the same: and in the third year sow ye, and reap, and plant vineyards, and eat the fruit thereof. 31 And the remnant that is escaped of the house of Judah shall again take root downward, and bear fruit upward: 32 For out of Jerusalem shall go forth a remnant, and they that escape out of mount Zion: the zeal of the Lord of hosts shall do this. 33 Therefore thus saith the Lord concerning the king of Assyria, He shall not come into this city, nor shoot an arrow there, nor come before it with shields, nor cast a bank against it. 34 By the way that he came, by the same shall he return, and shall not come into this city, saith the Lord. 35 For I will defend this city to save it for mine own sake, and for my servant David's sake.

37.30-35 To reassure the people God gives a sign of natural growth of their crops. As the land bears fruit, so shall the nation again bear fruit. God steps onto the stage at this time and informs Hezekiah, the King of Assyria will not enter the city of Jerusalem. Obedience to God demands God to intervene in the situation. God declares He will defend the city personally. The tables have now turned radically. It is no longer the Assyrians against Jerusalem, it is now the Assyrians against God. The outcome is no longer in doubt.

37.36-38 Then the angel of the Lord went forth, and smote in the camp of the Assyrians a hundred and fourscore and five thousand: and when they arose early in the morning, behold, they were all dead corpses. 37 So Sennacherib king of Assyria departed, and went and returned, and dwelt at Nineveh. 38 And it came to pass, as he was worshipping in the house of Nisroch his god, that Adrammelech and Sharezer his sons smote him with the sword; and they escaped into the land of Armenia: and Esarhaddon his son reigned in his stead.

37.36-38 This absolutely has to rank as one of the supreme moments of all recorded history. The mightiest army in the world stared down a weakened city. God rises from His throne and swats the Assyrian army like a man swats a gnat. 185,000 men died and were dead corpses as the dawn bathed the eastern sky.

Chapter 38

38.1-3 In those days was Hezekiah sick unto death. And Isaiah the prophet the son of Amoz came unto him, and said unto him, Thus saith the Lord, Set thine house in order: for thou shalt die, and not live. 2 Then Hezekiah turned his face toward the wall, and prayed unto the Lord, 3 And said, Remember now, O Lord, I beseech thee, how I have walked before thee in truth and with a perfect heart, and have done that which is good in thy sight. And Hezekiah wept sore.

38.1-3 Here we find the announcement of the impending death of King Hezekiah. This occurs at the same time as the beginning of the Assyrian invasion. Therefore King Hezekiah was in the fourteenth year of his reign. God adds fifteen years for a total time of twenty-nine years of Hezekiah's reign. Had he not been given more years, he would have died without an heir to the throne. This makes the event important enough to be written into sacred writ. His appeal to God to spare his life is a poignant moment of scripture. So much is hanging in the balance. Most importantly is King David's promised line to the messiah.

38.4-8 Then came the word of the Lord to Isaiah, saying,

5 Go, and say to Hezekiah, Thus saith the Lord, the God of David thy father, I have heard thy prayer, I have seen thy tears: behold, I will add unto thy days fifteen years. 6 And I will deliver thee and this city out of the hand of the king of Assyria: and I will defend this city. 7 And this shall be a sign unto thee from the Lord, that the Lord will do this thing that he hath spoken; 8 Behold, I will bring again the shadow of the degrees, which is gone down in the sun dial of Ahaz, ten degrees backward. So the sun returned ten degrees, by which degrees it was gone down.

38.4-8 God follows His normal protocol and speaks to Isaiah rather than directly to Hezekiah. This is the protocol throughout most of Biblical history. God speaks to His chosen mouthpieces, His ministers. Isaiah assures Hezekiah he will be healed and in addition, the city will be delivered. To solidify His word to the King, God gives an amazing sign. The sundial returns backward ten degrees. In 2 Ki 20.8 Hezekiah asks for a sign.

38.9-20 The writing of Hezekiah king of Judah, when he had been sick, and was recovered of his sickness: 10 I said in the cutting off of my days, I shall go to the gates of the grave: I am deprived of the residue of my years. 11 I said, I shall not see the Lord, even the Lord, in the land of the living: I shall behold man no more with the inhabitants of the world. 12 Mine age is departed, and is removed from me as a shepherd's tent: I have cut off like a weaver my life: he will cut me off with pining sickness: from day even to night wilt thou make an end of me. 13 I reckoned till morning, that, as a lion, so will he break all my bones: from day even to night wilt thou make an end of me. 14 Like a crane or a swallow, so did I chatter: I did mourn as a dove: mine eyes fail with looking upward: O Lord, I am oppressed; undertake for me. 15 What shall I say? he hath both spoken unto me, and himself hath done it: I shall go softly all my years in the bitterness of my soul. 16 O Lord, by these things men live, and in all these things is the life of my spirit: so wilt thou recover me, and make me to live. 17 Behold, for peace I had great bitterness: but thou hast in love to my soul delivered it from the pit of corruption: for thou hast cast all my sins behind thy back. 18 For the grave cannot praise thee, death can not celebrate thee: they that go down into the pit cannot hope for thy truth. 19 The living, the living, he shall praise thee, as I do this day: the father to the children shall make known thy truth. 20 The Lord was ready to save me: therefore we will sing my songs to the stringed instruments all the days of our life in the house of the Lord.

38.9-20 The michtam song of King Hezekiah. Michtam means golden psalm or song. Hezekiah had skirted death. He had walked to the edge of eternity and looked into the abyss. In a poetic way, this event is a national demonstration of Judah skirting death and looking into the abyss. Hezekiah was given a reprieve, and the nation also received additional national lifespan. As King Hezekiah rejoiced at his miracle of restored life and averted impending death, so the nation will also rejoice in the day of restoration and their coming messiah (Jesus), who restores the nation to life again. God uses the life of the most prominent man alive on planet earth, to show in living color, the parallel of His mercy to the nation.

38.21-22 For Isaiah had said, Let them take a lump of

figs, and lay it for a plaister upon the boil, and he shall recover. 22 Hezekiah also had said, What is the sign that I shall go up to the house of the Lord?

38. 21-22 The Spirit of God, the Holy Ghost, shows us a king and ruler of men, a dweller in palaces, a possessor of all that money can obtain, a good man, a friend of God, laid low by disease like the poorest man in the kingdom. His deliverance and cure comes by obedience to the prophet. The cure itself was nothing special. God so ordains that high or low, rich or poor, wise or unlearned, all men must have human leadership. It is through simple obedience, and attention to Isaiah's instruction, that healing, deliverance, and solution comes. This has ever been the plan of God. An anointed man to lead, instruct, and guide in our lives.

Chapter 39

39.1-3 At that time Merodachbaladan, the son of Baladan, king of Babylon, sent letters and a present to Hezekiah: for he had heard that he had been sick, and was recovered. 2 And Hezekiah was glad of them, and shewed them the house of his precious things, the silver, and the gold, and the spices, and the precious ointment, and all the house of his armour, and all that was found in his treasures: there was nothing in his house, nor in all his dominion, that Hezekiah shewed them not. 3 Then came Isaiah the prophet unto king Hezekiah, and said unto him, What said these men? and from whence came they unto thee? And Hezekiah said, They are come from a far country unto me, even from Babylon.

39.1-3 The story of life. .healed and saved in chapter 38, rebuked by the prophet in chapter 39. In Ch 38 God sends the prophet with words of life and sustenance. In ch 39 the same God sends the same preacher with words of harsh rebuke. In ch 38 a miracle, in ch 39 a mistake. In ch 38 a deliverance, in ch 39 a debacle. In ch 38 the promise of a reborn future. In ch 39 the promise of a radical fall. Hezekiah showed the world the mighty hand of God's supernatural healing, then turned right around and showed the world the secret treasures of God. So God sends the prophet again. This time the message is harsh and filled with horror. When you coquet with the son of the stranger, you invite the prophet's ire.

39.4 Then said he, What have they seen in thine house? And Hezekiah answered, All that is in mine house have they seen: there is nothing among my treasures that I have not shewed them.

39.4 What did they see?. The recently saved and delivered King, shows the enemy all. All the treasures and precious things. The knock on the door announcing the arrival of Isaiah ushers in a hush. Isaiah's face is stern and solemn. His words cascade like molten fire. Like lashes of the whip, Hezekiah is rebuked with words of future terror. What the Babylonians saw they will come back and pillage.

39.5-7 Then said Isaiah to Hezekiah, Hear the word of the Lord of hosts: 6 Behold, the days come, that all that is in thine house, and that which thy fathers have laid up in store until this day, shall be carried to Babylon: nothing shall be left, saith the Lord. 7 And of thy sons that shall issue from thee, which thou shalt beget, shall they take away; and they shall be eunuchs in the palace of the king of Babylon.

39.5-7 Isaiah sadly and vehemently informs the King, what has been gathered for generations will now be lost. All will be taken. Nothing shall be left saith the Lord. In addition to material things lost, your sons, the fruit of your own body will be enslaved. They shall be eunuchs and bare no sons. A last little bone is thrown to

Hezekiah. .It will not happen in your day. We should all be guardians of what it took generations to accumulate.

39.8 Then said Hezekiah to Isaiah, Good is the word of the Lord which thou hast spoken. He said moreover, For there shall be peace and truth in my days.

39.8 Hezekiah responds in a dual manner. First he accepts the judgment upon his actions as the edict of a righteous God. Then to our chagrin, he is comforted these events will not interrupt his peace. Over the kingdom of Judah there was now hanging the very same fate of captivity and exile, which had put an end to the kingdom of Israel. The end of the kingdom of Israel, and the beginning of the end of the kingdom of Judah, had their meeting-point in Hezekiah's reign. Hezekiah is content to push the coming calamity onto succeeding generations. In the great providence of God, this section of Isaiah, which alludes to the 39 books of the Old Testament, closes with judgment on the horizon. Chapter 40 is the dawn of a new day. In chapter 40, just as in the Gospel of Matthew, we are ushered into a brand new day. Even so, come Lord Jesus.

Chapter 40: Comfort, O Comfort My People

The prophet declares God's coming Glory contrasted with the people's helplessness. He encouraged the weary to count on the Lord's steadfast promises. Yahweh, the God of Eternity, the Creator of the earth, will comfort, care for and deliver them as the Great Shepherd of His sheep.

40.1-8 Comfort ye, comfort ye my people, saith your God. 2 Speak ye comfortably to Jerusalem, and cry unto her, that her warfare is accomplished, that her iniquity is pardoned: for she hath received of the Lord's hand double for all her sins. 3 The voice of him that crieth in the wilderness, Prepare ye the way of the Lord, make straight in the desert a highway for our God. 4 Every valley shall be exalted, and every mountain and hill shall be made low: and the crooked shall be made straight, and the rough places plain: 5 And the glory of the Lord shall be revealed, and all flesh shall see it together: for the mouth of the Lord hath spoken it. 6 The voice said, Cry. And he said, What shall I cry? All flesh is grass, and all the goodliness thereof is as the flower of the field: 7 The grass withereth, the flower fadeth: because the spirit of the Lord bloweth upon it:

surely the people is grass. 8 The grass withereth, the flower fadeth: but the word of our God shall stand for ever.

40.1-8 It is commonly described as the oldest manuscript of Isaiah found among the Dead Sea Scrolls. Isaiah foretells of the salvation coming and offers deep consolation to God's chosen people; consolation which will extend far beyond their Babylonian captivity. It appears that Isaiah is also describing a spiritual comfort that will only be achieved through repentance and by receiving the promised salvation to His people who live in covenant with Him. The voice of one crying in the wilderness is clearly speaking of John the Baptist, the one who would be a forerunner of Jesus Christ and proclaim for the world to behold the Lamb of God, which takes away the sins of the world. (Matt. 3.3, Mark 1:3, Luke 3:4, John 1:23.). The people are commanded to make their crooked paths straight and to smooth out the rough places to prepare for the foreordained coming of Messiah: Jesus Christ; God manifested in flesh (Is. 9:6; 1 Tim. 3:16.)

40.9-17 O Zion, that bringest good tidings, get thee up into the high mountain; O Jerusalem, that bringest good tidings, lift up thy voice with strength; lift it up, be not afraid; say unto the cities of Judah, Behold your God! 10 Behold, the Lord God will come with strong hand, and his arm shall rule for him: behold, his reward is with him, and his work before him. 11 He shall feed his flock like a shepherd: he shall gather the lambs with his arm, and carry them in his bosom, and shall gently lead those that are with young. 12 Who hath measured the waters in the hollow of his hand, and meted out heaven with the

span, and comprehended the dust of the earth in a measure, and weighed the mountains in scales, and the hills in a balance? 13 Who hath directed the Spirit of the Lord, or being his counsellor hath taught him? 14 With whom took he counsel, and who instructed him, and taught him in the path of judgment, and taught him knowledge, and shewed to him the way of understanding? 15 Behold, the nations are as a drop of a bucket, and are counted as the small dust of the balance: behold, he taketh up the isles as a very little thing. 16 And Lebanon is not sufficient to burn, nor the beasts thereof sufficient for a burnt offering. 17 All nations before him are as nothing; and they are counted to him less than nothing, and vanity.

40.9-17 The term O Zion, O Jerusalem puts focus upon the powerful City of David, which is resourced by God to help spread the good news throughout the cities of Judah. The Good News of the Gospel was first proclaimed in Jerusalem and the Apostolic New Birth message was first preached and experienced in this same city and spread to all the world beginning first at Jerusalem (Acts 1:4-8, 1:12-16, 2:1-47.). Behold your God! This refers to the coming of God in flesh: Jesus Christ was like a shepherd gathering his sheep (John 10.)

40.18-31 To whom then will ye liken God? or what likeness will ye compare unto him? 19 The workman melteth a graven image, and the goldsmith spreadeth it over with gold, and casteth silver chains. 20 He that is so impoverished that he hath no oblation chooseth a tree that will not rot; he seeketh unto him a cunning workman to prepare a graven image, that shall not be moved. 21 Have ye not known? have ye not heard?

hath it not been told you from the beginning? have ye not understood from the foundations of the earth? 22 It is he that sitteth upon the circle of the earth, and the inhabitants thereof are as grasshoppers; that stretcheth out the heavens as a curtain, and spreadeth them out as a tent to dwell in: 23 That bringeth the princes to nothing; he maketh the judges of the earth as vanity. 24 Yea, they shall not be planted; yea, they shall not be sown: yea, their stock shall not take root in the earth: and he shall also blow upon them, and they shall wither, and the whirlwind shall take them away as stubble. 25 To whom then will ye liken me, or shall I be equal? saith the Holy One. 26 Lift up your eyes on high, and behold who hath created these things, that bringeth out their host by number: he calleth them all by names by the greatness of his might, for that he is strong in power; not one faileth. 27 Why sayest thou, O Jacob, and speakest, O Israel, My way is hid from the Lord, and my judgment is passed over from my God? 28 Hast thou not known? hast thou not heard, that the everlasting God, the Lord, the Creator of the ends of the earth, fainteth not, neither is weary? there is no searching of his understanding. 29 He giveth power to the faint; and to them that have no might he increaseth strength. 30 Even the youths shall faint and be weary, and the young men shall utterly fall: 31 But they that wait upon the Lord shall renew their strength; they shall mount up with wings as eagles; they shall run, and not be weary; and they shall walk, and not faint.

40.18-31 Human idolatry in any form; whether in ancient times or modern times; is an absolute abomination and shameful in the sight of the Holy One of Israel. Through several questions in this section Isaiah helps call the audience to honor, worship and fear God. He further details that no idol mankind ever creates will compare to the All-powerful, All-knowing and Always-present, Sovereign One True God. Man is created in the image and likeness of God, not the other way around (Gen 1:27.)

Chapter 41: The Coming Deliverance

The prophet declares a threefold theme throughout chapters 40-66. Number one, God's people are in the Babylonian Captivity as a consequence of their adulterous hearts and wayward sins. Number two, this is also proving that God alone is the Only Sovereign God. After all, God predicted it. Number three, God alone will be the one to restore and redeem them from the captivity of sin. Forgiveness, redemption and deliverance is coming.

41.1-7 Keep silence before me, O islands; and let the people renew their strength: let them come near; then let them speak: let us come near together to judgment. 2 Who raised up the righteous man from the east, called him to his foot, gave the nations before him, and made him rule over kings? he gave them as the dust to his sword, and as driven stubble to his bow. 3 He pursued them, and passed safely; even by the way that he had not gone with his feet. 4 Who hath wrought and done it, calling the generations from the beginning? I the Lord, the first, and with the last; I am he. 5 The isles saw it, and feared; the ends of the earth were afraid, drew near, and came. 6 They helped every one his neighbour; and every one said to his brother,

Be of good courage. 7 So the carpenter encouraged the goldsmith, and he that smootheth with the hammer him that smote the anvil, saying, It is ready for the sodering: and he fastened it with nails, that it should not be moved.

41.1-7 The Lord called a ruler to fulfill His purposes. The righteous man from the east is speaking of the King Cyrus of Persia (558-529 B.C.) (Is. 44:28.). He was raised up from Persia to bring to pass the sovereign will of the One True God. No false gods or any other forms of idolatry had the power to do such a work. God's prophesied deliverance was facilitated and confirmed through the ruling decisions and favor received from Cyrus.

41.8-9 But thou, Israel, art my servant, Jacob whom I have chosen, the seed of Abraham my friend. 9 Thou whom I have taken from the ends of the earth, and called thee from the chief men thereof, and said unto thee, Thou art my servant; I have chosen thee, and not cast thee away.

41.8-9 Thou, Israel, art my servant is a reference to the Servant of the Lord, here pictured as the nation of Israel. The servant theme appears in numerous places of the beloved prophet's writings. At times, the term servant may mean an individual Israelite (Is 22:20), at other times it may refer to the nation of Israel (Is 41:8), or it may refer to the believing remnant (49:3) and it also clearly refers to the promised Messiah (Is 52:13) The term servant is a slave or bondman, in this context has an honorable connotation which speaks of the close intimacy between master and servant. The prophet uses the servant terminology to foretell of Messiah's redemptive works as the suffering Servant (52:13-53:12.)

41.10-20 Fear thou not; for I am with thee: be not dismayed; for I am thy God: I will strengthen thee; yea, I will help thee; yea, I will uphold thee with the right hand of my righteousness. 11 Behold, all they that were incensed against thee shall be ashamed and confounded: they shall be as nothing; and they that strive with thee shall perish. 12 Thou shalt seek them, and shalt not find them, even them that contended with thee: they that war against thee shall be as nothing, and as a thing of nought. 13 For I the Lord thy God will hold thy right hand, saying unto thee, Fear not; I will help thee. 14 Fear not, thou worm Jacob, and ye men of Israel; I will help thee, saith the Lord, and thy redeemer, the Holy One of Israel. 15 Behold, I will make thee a new sharp threshing instrument having teeth: thou shalt thresh the mountains, and beat them small, and shalt make the hills as chaff. 16 Thou shalt fan them, and the wind shall carry them away, and the whirlwind shall scatter them: and thou shalt rejoice in the Lord, and shalt glory in the Holy One of Israel. 17 When the poor and needy seek water, and there is none, and their tongue faileth for thirst, I the Lord will hear them, I the God of Israel will not forsake them. 18 I will open rivers in high places, and fountains in the midst of the valleys: I will make the wilderness a pool of water, and the dry land springs of water. 19 I will plant in the wilderness the cedar, the shittah tree, and the myrtle, and the oil tree; I will set in the desert the fir tree, and the pine, and the box tree together: 20 That they may see, and know, and consider, and understand together, that the hand of the Lord hath done this, and the Holy One of Israel hath created it.

41.10-20 God reminds the nation of Israel that He is with her and that He alone is worthy to be her God. The designation thou worm Jacob is a reminder to Israel of her frailty and need for God who is her redeemer and the Holy One of Israel. The term Holy One of Israel is used often by the prophet to describe the One True God throughout his prophecy. The prophet gives a descriptive visual of God abundantly supplying the basic needs of His people. God promises to provide for them rivers, fountains and springs of waters. There are seven types of trees mentioned by the prophet, which were commonly found throughout the region. God's number of perfection may be seen as symbolic of God's perfectly ordered work of redemption and the perfect provision on behalf of His people.

41.21-29 Produce your cause, saith the Lord; bring forth your strong reasons, saith the King of Jacob. 22 Let them bring them forth, and shew us what shall happen: let them shew the former things, what they be, that we may consider them, and know the latter end of them; or declare us things for to come. 23 Shew the things that are to come hereafter, that we may know that ye are gods: yea, do good, or do evil, that we may be dismayed, and behold it together. 24 Behold, ye are of nothing, and your work of nought: an abomination is he that chooseth you. 25 I have raised up one from the north, and he shall come: from the rising of the sun shall he call upon my name: and he shall come upon princes as upon morter, and as the potter treadeth clay. 26 Who hath declared from the beginning, that we may know? and beforetime, that we may say, He is righteous? yea, there is none that sheweth, yea, there is none that declareth, yea, there is none that heareth your words. 27 The first

shall say to Zion, Behold, behold them: and I will give to Jerusalem one that bringeth good tidings. 28 For I beheld, and there was no man; even among them, and there was no counsellor, that, when I asked of them, could answer a word. 29 Behold, they are all vanity; their works are nothing: their molten images are wind and confusion.

41.21-29 The Lord challenges the gods of the heathen nations to produce their cause and to bring forth their strong reasons. God challenged the idol gods directly. Did they predict the future events?. No; furthermore, they had not said anything at all, for they had no ability. All of the false gods of idolatry stood speechless and had no power before the Holy One of Israel. Isaiah declared for Israel to not fear, for Israel was the chosen servant of God. The Law of Moses (Duet 18:21-22) gives the requirement for the fulfillment of predictive prophecy as evidence of the Divine Authority and genuineness of the Prophet's message.

Chapter 42: The Role of God's Servant

The Servant introduced in the prophet's writings is the suffering Servant fulfilling the foreordained plan. The Servant Jesus Christ ushered in the Kingdom of God in an unexpected manner and achieved powerful results as the promised Messiah (Matt. 12:18-21.). The powerful supernatural workings of miracles, signs and wonders were done by our meek and lowly Redeemer Jesus Christ; God manifested in flesh (Matt. 1:23, 1 Tim. 3:16.)

42.1-4 Behold my servant, whom I uphold; mine elect, in whom my soul delighteth; I have put my spirit upon him: he shall bring forth judgment to the Gentiles. 2 He shall not cry, nor lift up, nor cause his voice to be heard in the street. 3 A bruised reed shall he not break, and the smoking flax shall he not quench: he shall bring forth judgment unto truth. 4 He shall not fail nor be discouraged, till he have set judgment in the earth: and the isles shall wait for his law.

42.1-4 My servant is identified here as Israel's King, Prophet, High Priest and mine elect set apart for the purpose of Redemption. This is clearly speaking of Messiah, Jesus Christ Himself. The Gospel according to

Matthew declares this was fulfilled in the Lord Jesus Christ; God manifested in flesh (Matt. 12:18-21.). The Servant of the Lord's Kingdom would not be limited to only the House Israel; there would be no barriers of nationality or race; thankfully, His Ministry and work of Salvation was also extended to the Gentiles; thus the whole world.

42.5-16 Thus saith God the Lord, he that created the heavens, and stretched them out; he that spread forth the earth, and that which cometh out of it; he that giveth breath unto the people upon it, and spirit to them that walk therein: 6 I the Lord have called thee in righteousness, and will hold thine hand, and will keep thee, and give thee for a covenant of the people, for a light of the Gentiles; 7 To open the blind eyes, to bring out the prisoners from the prison, and them that sit in darkness out of the prison house. 8 I am the Lord: that is my name: and my glory will I not give to another, neither my praise to graven images. 9 Behold, the former things are come to pass, and new things do I declare: before they spring forth I tell you of them. 10 Sing unto the Lord a new song, and his praise from the end of the earth, ye that go down to the sea, and all that is therein; the isles, and the inhabitants thereof. 11 Let the wilderness and the cities thereof lift up their voice, the villages that Kedar doth inhabit: let the inhabitants of the rock sing, let them shout from the top of the mountains. 12 Let them give glory unto the Lord, and declare his praise in the islands. 13 The Lord shall go forth as a mighty man, he shall stir up jealousy like a man of war: he shall cry, yea, roar; he shall prevail against his enemies. 14 I have long time holden my peace; I have been still, and refrained myself: now will I cry like a travailing woman; I will

destroy and devour at once. 15 I will make waste mountains and hills, and dry up all their herbs; and I will make the rivers islands, and I will dry up the pools. 16 And I will bring the blind by a way that they knew not; I will lead them in paths that they have not known: I will make darkness light before them, and crooked things straight. These things will I do unto them, and not forsake them.

42.5-16 Israel and Judah should have been a light for the Gentiles, but they were actually blind and desperately needed a Savior. The Ministry of the Messiah Jesus Christ was a covenant to the Jews and a light to the Gentiles. God Almighty is the Creator of the heavens and the earth. This Almighty God, also gives breath and spirit to His people.

42.17-25 They shall be turned back, they shall be greatly ashamed, that trust in graven images, that say to the molten images, Ye are our gods. 18 Hear, ye deaf; and look, ye blind, that ye may see. 19 Who is blind, but my servant? or deaf, as my messenger that I sent? who is blind as he that is perfect, and blind as the Lord's servant? 20 Seeing many things, but thou observest not; opening the ears, but he heareth not. 21 The Lord is well pleased for his righteousness' sake; he will magnify the law, and make it honourable. 22 But this is a people robbed and spoiled; they are all of them snared in holes, and they are hid in prison houses: they are for a prey, and none delivereth; for a spoil, and none saith, Restore. 23 Who among you will give ear to this? who will hearken and hear for the time to come? 24 Who gave Jacob for a spoil, and Israel to the robbers? did not the Lord, he against whom we have sinned? for they would not walk in his ways, neither were they obedient unto his law. 25 Therefore he hath poured upon him the fury of his anger, and the strength of battle: and it hath set him on fire round about, yet he knew not; and it burned him, yet he laid it not to heart.

42.17-25 Christ's faithful Servant-hood example is a striking contrast to Israel's role as God's blind, deaf, and unfaithful servant. The nation of Israel repeatedly and adulterously disobeyed God's Laws, she ignored His prophets and preachers, and consequently, she paid the high price of God's judgment with her painful exile in Babylon.

Chapter 43: The Redemption of Israel from Babylon

Isaiah described God's power and blessing. Although, Israel clearly displayed a rebellious attitude from the very beginning in her relationship with God, The Holy One of Israel would become their Savior and Redeemer, and He would lead them to them home from the devastation of exile in a strange land.

43.1-13 But now thus saith the Lord that created thee, O Jacob, and he that formed thee, O Israel, Fear not: for I have redeemed thee, I have called thee by thy name; thou art mine. 2 When thou passest through the waters, I will be with thee; and through the rivers, they shall not overflow thee: when thou walkest through the fire, thou shalt not be burned; neither shall the flame kindle upon thee. 3 For I am the Lord thy God, the Holy One of Israel, thy Saviour: I gave Egypt for thy ransom, Ethiopia and Seba for thee. 4 Since thou wast precious in my sight, thou hast been honourable, and I have loved thee: therefore will I give men for thee, and people for thy life. 5 Fear not: for I am with thee: I will bring thy seed from the east, and gather thee from the west; 6 I will say to the north, Give up; and to the south, Keep not back: bring my sons from far, and my daughters from the ends of the earth; 7 Even every one that is called by my name: for I have created him for my glory, I have formed him; yea, I have made him. 8 Bring forth the blind people that have eyes, and the deaf that have ears. 9 Let all the nations be gathered together, and let the people be assembled: who among them can declare this, and shew us former things? let them bring forth their witnesses, that they may be justified: or let them hear, and say, It is truth. 10 Ye are my witnesses, saith the Lord, and my servant whom I have chosen: that ye may know and believe me, and understand that I am he: before me there was no God formed, neither shall there be after me. 11 I, even I, am the Lord; and beside me there is no saviour. 12 I have declared, and have saved, and I have shewed, when there was no strange god among you: therefore ye are my witnesses, saith the Lord, that I am God. 13 Yea, before the day was I am he; and there is none that can deliver out of my hand: I will work, and who shall let it?

43.1-13 The only Savior for Judah will be the Lord Himself. He will be with them as they go through the deep waters and fire; but the floodwaters shall not destroy them and the fire shall not consume them. God will save Israel. This great promise of God will be fulfilled at several levels. Number one, the prophecy of exile in to Babylon, afterward many of God's people will be restored to the land through the leadership of God's prophets Ezra, Nehemiah, and others. Number two, following the coming of Messiah Jesus Christ and the outpouring of the Holy Ghost upon the church, God's people will be gathered to the Lord. Lastly, at the return and second coming of the Jesus Christ, all of God's people will be gathered to the Lord forever. The theme of redemption appears 22 times in the Servant passages of the Book of Isaiah. It indicates a redemption from physical and spiritual bondage as well as the eschatological redemption yet to come (Is. 43:5-7, 44:22, 49:16.).

43.14-28 Thus saith the Lord, your redeemer, the Holy One of Israel; For your sake I have sent to Babylon, and have brought down all their nobles, and the Chaldeans, whose cry is in the ships. 15 I am the Lord, your Holy One, the creator of Israel, your King. 16 Thus saith the Lord, which maketh a way in the sea, and a path in the mighty waters; 17 Which bringeth forth the chariot and horse, the army and the power; they shall lie down together, they shall not rise: they are extinct, they are quenched as tow. 18 Remember ye not the former things, neither consider the things of old. 19 Behold, I will do a new thing; now it shall spring forth; shall ye not know it? I will even make a way in the wilderness, and rivers in the desert. 20 The beast of the field shall honour me, the dragons and the owls: because I give waters in the wilderness, and rivers in the desert, to give drink to my people, my chosen. 21 This people have I formed for myself; they shall shew forth my praise. 22 But thou hast not called upon me, O Jacob; but thou hast been weary of me, O Israel. 23 Thou hast not brought me the small cattle of thy burnt offerings; neither hast thou honoured me with thy sacrifices. I have not caused thee to serve with an offering, nor wearied thee with incense. 24 Thou hast bought me no sweet cane with money, neither hast thou filled me with the fat of thy sacrifices: but thou hast made me to serve with thy sins, thou hast wearied me with thine iniquities. 25 I, even I, am he that blotteth out thy transgressions for

mine own sake, and will not remember thy sins. 26 Put me in remembrance: let us plead together: declare thou, that thou mayest be justified. 27 Thy first father hath sinned, and thy teachers have transgressed against me. 28 Therefore I have profaned the princes of the sanctuary, and have given Jacob to the curse, and Israel to reproaches.

43.14-28 Before the people go into captivity, God assures them of their release. The Israelites held their deliverance from Egypt as the benchmark of deliverance. He predicts that God will judge Israel. But the prophet is declaring that God will do a new work of deliverance that will prove to be far greater. Isaiah combines the titles redeemer and Holy One of Israel as the One who shall overcome Babylon and the Chaldeans. It appears that God received more honor from unclean animals like jackals and owls than His chosen people who were supposed to faithfully worship Him. After the exile, the Children of Israel are clearly expected to be more faithful and appreciative of His love.

Chapter 44: Proclaiming The One True God's Redemption and Sovereignty

Isaiah declared the One True God of Israel as the only Savior and Redeemer. Without water there is no life; we are dead in sins and trespasses and without the promise God's Spirit there is no spiritual life possible. God Himself proclaimed through Isaiah's writing that He was superior to all idols. In fact, the convicting message questioned how could His chosen people bow down to idols crafted with their own hands?. They had clearly ignored His laws, statues and commands (Lev. 19:4, Lev. 26:1, Deut. 29:17, Is. 2:8, 18-20.) It made no sense then, and today, in the promised days of the Holy Ghost outpouring (Joel 2: 27-29, Acts 2:16-18), neither does any form of idolatry, false doctrines, erroneous teachings and spiritual apostasy characteristic of the last days prior to the second coming of our Redeemer and Savior for His called, chosen and faithful people (2 Tim 3:1-5, 2 Pet 3:1-18, Heb. 1:1-8, Rev. 17:14.)

44.1-8 Yet now hear, O Jacob my servant; and Israel, whom I have chosen: 2 Thus saith the Lord that made thee, and formed thee from the womb, which will help thee; Fear not, O Jacob, my servant; and thou, Jesurun, whom I have chosen. 3 For I will pour water upon him

that is thirsty, and floods upon the dry ground: I will pour my spirit upon thy seed, and my blessing upon thine offspring: 4 And they shall spring up as among the grass, as willows by the water courses. 5 One shall say, I am the Lord's; and another shall call himself by the name of Jacob; and another shall subscribe with his hand unto the Lord, and surname himself by the name of Israel. 6 Thus saith the Lord the King of Israel, and his redeemer the Lord of hosts; I am the first, and I am the last; and beside me there is no God. 7 And who, as I, shall call, and shall declare it, and set it in order for me, since I appointed the ancient people? and the things that are coming, and shall come, let them shew unto them. 8 Fear ye not, neither be afraid: have not I told thee from that time, and have declared it? ye are even my witnesses. Is there a God beside me? yea, there is no God; I know not any.

44.1-8 Once again, Israel is described as His servant chosen to fulfill God's purposes. God teaches that without the Spirit of God, people will remain spiritually dead in sins. Our beloved Monotheistic prophet, emphatically and clearly declares the Oneness of God stating that He is the First and He is the Last (Col. 1: 14-20, Rev. 1:11, 17, Rev. 2:8, Rev. 22:13) and beside me there is no God (Deut. 6:4, Mal. 2:10, Mark 12:29-32, Rom. 3:30, I Cor. 8:6, Eph. 4:6, 1 Tim. 2:5, James 2:19.). The foretelling almost a century and a half in advance, King Cyrus of Persia, is clearly described as the ruler whereby through his actions and decisions God would deliverer the Israelites. God's only name Yahweh is used to describe both their Sovereign King and their promised Mighty Redeemer (Col. 1:12-22, 1 Tim. 3:16.)

44.9-20 They that make a graven image are all of them

vanity; and their delectable things shall not profit; and they are their own witnesses; they see not, nor know; that they may be ashamed. 10 Who hath formed a god, or molten a graven image that is profitable for nothing? 11 Behold, all his fellows shall be ashamed: and the workmen, they are of men: let them all be gathered together, let them stand up; yet they shall fear, and they shall be ashamed together. 12 The smith with the tongs both worketh in the coals, and fashioneth it with hammers, and worketh it with the strength of his arms: yea, he is hungry, and his strength faileth: he drinketh no water, and is faint. 13 The carpenter stretcheth out his rule; he marketh it out with a line; he fitteth it with planes, and he marketh it out with the compass, and maketh it after the figure of a man, according to the beauty of a man; that it may remain in the house. 14 He heweth him down cedars, and taketh the cypress and the oak, which he strengtheneth for himself among the trees of the forest: he planteth an ash, and the rain doth nourish it. 15 Then shall it be for a man to burn: for he will take thereof, and warm himself; yea, he kindleth it, and baketh bread; yea, he maketh a god, and worshippeth it; he maketh it a graven image, and falleth down thereto. 16 He burneth part thereof in the fire; with part thereof he eateth flesh; he roasteth roast, and is satisfied: yea, he warmeth himself, and saith, Aha, I am warm, I have seen the fire: 17 And the residue thereof he maketh a god, even his graven image: he falleth down unto it, and worshippeth it, and prayeth unto it, and saith, Deliver me; for thou art my god. 18 They have not known nor understood: for he hath shut their eyes, that they cannot see; and their hearts, that they cannot understand. 19 And none considereth in his heart, neither is there knowledge nor understanding to say, I have burned part of it in the fire; yea, also I have baked bread upon the coals thereof; I have roasted flesh, and eaten it: and shall I make the residue thereof an abomination? shall I fall down to the stock of a tree? 20 He feedeth on ashes: a deceived heart hath turned him aside, that he cannot deliver his soul, nor say, Is there not a lie in my right hand?

44.9-20 Isaiah speaking on behalf of the One God Yahweh, clearly declares the absolute sinfulness and foolishness of polytheistic idolatry. Paganism is rightly ascribed to be futile and meaningless. Furthermore, he condemns and preaches conviction regarding adorning idols with gold, silver and precious stones. The objects of vanity are profitable for nothing and are partly confirmed to be so by the exercised faculty of reason; in that: who with good sense worships an idol carved from the same tree that is used for cooking and heating fuel on a cold day?

44.21-28 Remember these, O Jacob and Israel; for thou art my servant: I have formed thee; thou art my servant: O Israel, thou shalt not be forgotten of me. 22 I have blotted out, as a thick cloud, thy transgressions, and, as a cloud, thy sins: return unto me; for I have redeemed thee. 23 Sing, O ye heavens; for the Lord hath done it: shout, ye lower parts of the earth: break forth into singing, ye mountains, O forest, and every tree therein: for the Lord hath redeemed Jacob, and glorified himself in Israel. 24 Thus saith the Lord, thy redeemer, and he that formed thee from the womb, I am the Lord that maketh all things; that stretcheth forth the heavens alone; that spreadeth abroad the earth by myself; 25 That frustrateth the tokens of the liars, and maketh diviners mad; that turneth

wise men backward, and maketh their knowledge foolish; 26 That confirmeth the word of his servant, and performeth the counsel of his messengers; that saith to Jerusalem, Thou shalt be inhabited; and to the cities of Judah, Ye shall be built, and I will raise up the decayed places thereof: 27 That saith to the deep, Be dry, and I will dry up thy rivers: 28 That saith of Cyrus, He is my shepherd, and shall perform all my pleasure: even saying to Jerusalem, Thou shalt be built; and to the temple, Thy foundation shall be laid.

44.21-28 God alone blotted out Israel's transgressions and redeemed them; Isaiah urged them to repent and return to walk in His ways. The beautiful One God message of I am the Lord and the Creator of all things is emphasized again (Is 44:1-8) and the works of the Lord are identified. Jerusalem shall be inhabited by God's chosen people and the cities of Judah shall be built again. God promised to raise up Cyrus as deliverer. Cyrus the Great conquered Babylon (539 B.C.) and decreed the return of the Jews to rebuild Jerusalem and the temple (Ezra 1:2.)

Chapter 45: The One and Only True God

It was God who went before King Cyrus to level mountains, tear down gates and to facilitate the accumulation of the great wealth in his kingdom. Anyone who opposed Cyrus was in effect arguing with God. One day every knee will bow to this Mighty God named Yahweh (Is. 45:23, Rom. 14:11, Philip. 2:9-11.)

45.1-12 Thus saith the Lord to his anointed, to Cyrus, whose right hand I have holden, to subdue nations before him; and I will loose the loins of kings, to open before him the two leaved gates; and the gates shall not be shut; 2 I will go before thee, and make the crooked places straight: I will break in pieces the gates of brass, and cut in sunder the bars of iron: 3 And I will give thee the treasures of darkness, and hidden riches of secret places, that thou mayest know that I, the Lord, which call thee by thy name, am the God of Israel. 4 For Jacob my servant's sake, and Israel mine elect, I have even called thee by thy name: I have surnamed thee, though thou hast not known me. 5 I am the Lord, and there is none else, there is no God beside me: I girded thee, though thou hast not known me: 6 That they may know from the rising of the sun, and from the west, that there is none beside me. I am the Lord,

and there is none else. 7 I form the light, and create darkness: I make peace, and create evil: I the Lord do all these things. 8 Drop down, ye heavens, from above, and let the skies pour down righteousness: let the earth open, and let them bring forth salvation, and let righteousness spring up together; I the Lord have created it. 9 Woe unto him that striveth with his Maker! Let the potsherd strive with the potsherds of the earth. Shall the clay say to him that fashioneth it, What makest thou? or thy work, He hath no hands? 10 Woe unto him that saith unto his father, What begettest thou? or to the woman, What hast thou brought forth? 11 Thus saith the Lord, the Holy One of Israel, and his Maker, Ask me of things to come concerning my sons, and concerning the work of my hands command ye me. 12 I have made the earth, and created man upon it: I, even my hands, have stretched out the heavens, and all their host have I commanded.

45.1-12 Isaiah declares that Yahweh Himself has opened the door of expansion and dominion for the anointed King Cyrus. The Persian King is anointed in the context of being used to accomplish the foretold Holy One of Israel's sovereign purpose of miraculously delivering His chosen people. It was declared, Yahweh alone is the Creator and Redeemer; He is the All-powerful, All-knowing and Always-present, Sovereign One True God (Is. 7:4, Is. 9:6-7, Is. 12:4, Matt. 1:18-23, Luke 1:30-33, Philip. 2:9-11, Heb. 13:8.). As the Creator of heaven and Earth, God Almighty was the perfect architect in the revealed plans of redemption (Duet. 29:25-29, Matt. 13:35, Matt. 25:34, Heb. 4:3, Rev. 13:8.)

45.13-19 I have raised him up in righteousness, and I will direct all his ways: he shall build my city, and he

shall let go my captives, not for price nor reward, saith the Lord of hosts. 14 Thus saith the Lord, The labour of Egypt, and merchandise of Ethiopia and of the Sabeans, men of stature, shall come over unto thee, and they shall be thine: they shall come after thee; in chains they shall come over, and they shall fall down unto thee, they shall make supplication unto thee, saying, Surely God is in thee; and there is none else, there is no God. 15 Verily thou art a God that hidest thyself, O God of Israel, the Saviour. 16 They shall be ashamed, and also confounded, all of them: they shall go to confusion together that are makers of idols. 17 But Israel shall be saved in the Lord with an everlasting salvation: ye shall not be ashamed nor confounded world without end. 18 For thus saith the Lord that created the heavens; God himself that formed the earth and made it; he hath established it, he created it not in vain, he formed it to be inhabited: I am the Lord; and there is none else. 19 I have not spoken in secret, in a dark place of the earth: I said not unto the seed of Jacob, Seek ye me in vain: I the Lord speak righteousness, I declare things that are right.

45.13-19 The prophet Isaiah again boldly proclaims that King Cyrus is being raised up in the righteousness of God's purpose to free the exiled captives and to ultimately facilitate the promised return home for rebuilding the Lord's beloved city of Jerusalem, and His temple (Ezra 1:1-11.)

45.20-25 Assemble yourselves and come; draw near together, ye that are escaped of the nations: they have no knowledge that set up the wood of their graven image, and pray unto a god that cannot save. 21 Tell ye, and bring them near; yea, let them take counsel together: who hath declared this from ancient time? who hath told it from that time? have not I the Lord? and there is no God else beside me; a just God and a Saviour; there is none beside me. 22 Look unto me, and be ye saved, all the ends of the earth: for I am God, and there is none else. 23 I have sworn by myself, the word is gone out of my mouth in righteousness, and shall not return, That unto me every knee shall bow, every tongue shall swear. 24 Surely, shall one say, in the Lord have I righteousness and strength: even to him shall men come; and all that are incensed against him shall be ashamed. 25 In the Lord shall all the seed of Israel be justified, and shall glory.

45.20-25 Yahweh will be the Savior to those who will come to Him. Look unto me and be saved all the ends of the earth is a glorious invitation to all nations and peoples to come to the Lord for salvation. It was clearly fulfilled in the declaration of Jesus being both the son of man AND the Son of God; God manifested in flesh born to fulfill all things and to bring the forgiveness and remission of sins, the promised rest in the Holy Ghost made available to all nations and peoples of the earth beginning first at Jerusalem (Matt 3:17, Matt. 11:28, Matt. 17:5, Mark 1:11, Luke 4:14-21, Luke 4:43, Phil. 2:10, 1 Cor. 6:9-11, Col. 1:12-22, 1 Tim. 3:16, 2 Pet. 1:16-21.). The beloved prophet boldly confirms that only in the Lord shall the seed of Israel be justified and saved (Rom. 11:25-27, Rom. 11:32-36.)

Chapter 46:. The beloved prophet predicts the fall of Babylon to the conquest of Persia

Describing the striking and obvious superiority of the One God of Israel as compared to the useless multitude of false gods of the idolatrous Babylonian kingdom. The idols cowered as they could not redeem nor save Babylon from destruction; but the God of Israel will redeem and save the remnant of Israel in Zion from the womb all the way to His glory.

46.1-13 Bel boweth down, Nebo stoopeth, their idols were upon the beasts, and upon the cattle: your carriages were heavy loaden; they are a burden to the weary beast. 2 They stoop, they bow down together; they could not deliver the burden, but themselves are gone into captivity. 3 Hearken unto me, O house of Jacob, and all the remnant of the house of Israel, which are borne by me from the belly, which are carried from the womb: 4 And even to your old age I am he; and even to hoar hairs will I carry you: I have made, and I will bear; even I will carry, and will deliver you. 5 To whom will ye liken me, and make me equal, and compare me, that we may be like? 6

They lavish gold out of the bag, and weigh silver in the balance, and hire a goldsmith; and he maketh it a god: they fall down, yea, they worship. 7 They bear him upon the shoulder, they carry him, and set him in his place, and he standeth; from his place shall he not remove: yea, one shall cry unto him, yet can he not answer, nor save him out of his trouble. 8 Remember this, and shew yourselves men: bring it again to mind, O ye transgressors. 9 Remember the former things of old: for I am God, and there is none else; I am God, and there is none like me, 10 Declaring the end from the beginning, and from ancient times the things that are not yet done, saying, My counsel shall stand, and I will do all my pleasure: 11 Calling a ravenous bird from the east, the man that executeth my counsel from a far country: yea, I have spoken it, I will also bring it to pass; I have purposed it, I will also do it. 12 Hearken unto me, ye stouthearted, that are far from righteousness: 13 I bring near my righteousness; it shall not be far off, and my salvation shall not tarry: and I will place salvation in Zion for Israel my glory.

46.1-13 Historically, two of the most prominent Babylonian deities were known as Bel and Nebo. Yet, they are both like all forms of idolatry, useless and detestable before God. (Micah 5:2-4, 2 Cor. 6:14-18.). The prophet asks the question to whom will ye liken me? There is none like the Lord. Yahweh alone is God, and there is none before, beside or after Him; declaring the end from the beginning.

Thus, the salvation of the Lord shall not be delayed or stopped (Hab. 2:2-4, Heb. 10:34-39.). In God's sovereign will all things are unfolded in His precise and perfect timing and under His providence. Ultimately, it is the high calling of God's people to reverently bring their humble lives into complete covenantal agreement with His Word, Spirit and Name; for it is only through these; whereby, we may experience God's love through His perfect work of justification, sanctification and glorification (1 Cor. 1: 18-31, 1 Pet. 2:1-10, 1 John 3:1-5.)

Chapter 47

47.1-15 Come down, and sit in the dust, O virgin daughter of Babylon, sit on the ground: there is no throne, O daughter of the Chaldeans: for thou shalt no more be called tender and delicate. 2 Take the millstones, and grind meal: uncover thy locks, make bare the leg, uncover the thigh, pass over the rivers. 3 Thy nakedness shall be uncovered, yea, thy shame shall be seen: I will take vengeance, and I will not meet thee as a man. 4 As for our redeemer, the Lord of hosts is his name, the Holy One of Israel. 5 Sit thou silent, and get thee into darkness, O daughter of the Chaldeans: for thou shalt no more be called, The lady of kingdoms. 6 I was wroth with my people, I have polluted mine inheritance, and given them into thine hand: thou didst shew them no mercy; upon the ancient hast thou very heavily laid thy yoke. 7 And thou saidst, I shall be a lady for ever: so that thou didst not lay these things to thy heart, neither didst remember the latter end of it. 8 Therefore hear now this, thou that art given to pleasures, that dwellest carelessly, that sayest in thine heart, I am, and none else beside me; I shall not sit as a widow, neither shall I know the loss of children: 9 But these two things shall come to thee in a moment in one day, the loss of children, and widowhood: they shall come upon thee in their perfection for the multitude of thy sorceries, and for the great abundance of thine enchantments. 10 For thou hast trusted in thy wickedness: thou hast said, None seeth me. Thy wisdom and thy knowledge, it hath perverted thee; and thou hast said in thine heart, I am, and none else beside me. 11 Therefore shall evil come upon thee; thou shalt not know from whence it riseth: and mischief shall fall upon thee; thou shalt not be able to put it off: and desolation shall come upon thee suddenly, which thou shalt not know. 12 Stand now with thine enchantments, and with the multitude of thy sorceries, wherein thou hast laboured from thy youth; if so be thou shalt be able to profit, if so be thou mayest prevail. 13 Thou art wearied in the multitude of thy counsels. Let now the astrologers, the stargazers, the monthly prognosticators, stand up, and save thee from these things that shall come upon thee. 14 Behold, they shall be as stubble; the fire shall burn them; they shall not deliver themselves from the power of the flame: there shall not be a coal to warm at, nor fire to sit before it. 15 Thus shall they be unto thee with whom thou hast laboured, even thy merchants, from thy youth: they shall wander every one to his quarter; none shall save thee.

47.1-15 Isaiah now pictures Babylon as an ousted queen who can do no more that sit in the dust. In spite of its splendor, ancient Babylon was built upon the dust of the desert of Shinar. The Chaldeans were the elite ruling class of the Neo-Babylonian Empire. In this passage Babylon is pictured as a naked slave girl reduced to sitting in the dust. She is no longer the lady [mistress] of kingdoms. This same imagery is found in Revelation, where Babylon is called the "great whore" (17:1; 19:2; cf. 18:3).

Chapter 48

48.1-11 Hear ye this, O house of Jacob, which are called by the name of Israel, and are come forth out of the waters of Judah, which swear by the name of the Lord, and make mention of the God of Israel, but not in truth, nor in righteousness. 2 For they call themselves of the holy city, and stay themselves upon the God of Israel; The Lord of hosts is his name. 3 I have declared the former things from the beginning; and they went forth out of my mouth, and I shewed them; I did them suddenly, and they came to pass. 4 Because I knew that thou art obstinate, and thy neck is an iron sinew, and thy brow brass; 5 I have even from the beginning declared it to thee; before it came to pass I shewed it thee: lest thou shouldest say, Mine idol hath done them, and my graven image, and my molten image, hath commanded them. 6 Thou hast heard, see all this; and will not ye declare it? I have shewed thee new things from this time, even hidden things, and thou didst not know them. 7 They are created now, and not from the beginning; even before the day when thou heardest them not; lest thou shouldest say, Behold, I knew them. 8 Yea, thou heardest not; yea, thou knewest not; yea, from that time that thine ear was not opened: for I knew that thou wouldest deal very treacherously, and wast called a transgressor from the womb. 9 For my name's sake will I defer mine anger, and for my praise will I refrain for thee, that I cut thee not off. 10 Behold, I have refined thee, but not with silver; I have chosen thee in the furnace of affliction. 11 For mine own sake, even for mine own sake, will I do it: for how should my name be polluted? and I will not give my glory unto another.

48.1-11 The house of Jacob includes both Israel and Judah. God often finds His people obstinate and perverse, but for all that He makes it redound to the honor of His mercy to spare and pardon them, refining them in the furnace of affliction, rather than cutting them off. I have chosen [tried] thee in the furnace of affliction refers to God's merciful judgment, which has burned away their dross. (Isa 4:4)

48.12-22 Hearken unto me, O Jacob and Israel, my called; I am he; I am the first, I also am the last. 13 Mine hand also hath laid the foundation of the earth, and my right hand hath spanned the heavens: when I call unto them, they stand up together. 14 All ye, assemble yourselves, and hear; which among them hath declared these things? The Lord hath loved him: he will do his pleasure on Babylon, and his arm shall be on the Chaldeans. 15 I, even I, have spoken; yea, I have called him: I have brought him, and he shall make his way prosperous. 16 Come ye near unto me, hear ye this; I have not spoken in secret from the beginning; from the time that it was, there am I: and now the Lord God, and his Spirit, hath sent me. 17 Thus saith the Lord, thy Redeemer, the Holy One of Israel; I am the Lord thy God which teacheth thee to profit, which leadeth thee by the way that thou shouldest go. 18 O that thou hadst hearkened to my commandments! then had thy peace been as a river, and thy righteousness as the waves of the sea: 19 Thy seed also had been as the sand, and the offspring of thy bowels like the gravel thereof; his name should not have been cut off nor destroyed from before me. 20 Go ye forth of Babylon, flee ye from the Chaldeans, with a voice of singing declare ye, tell this, utter it even to the end of the earth; say ye, The Lord hath redeemed his servant Jacob.21 And they thirsted not when he led them through the deserts: he caused the waters to flow out of the rock for them: he clave the rock also, and the waters gushed out. 22 There is no peace, saith the Lord, unto the wicked.

48.12-22 In spite of their failures, both Jacob and Israel are still called and chosen by God. He is their LORD, thy Redeemer, the Holy One of Israel, reaffirming that He is the first and last, the I AM will lead them. (John 8:24; Rev 1:8, 11, 17)

Chapter 49

49.1-6 Listen, O isles, unto me; and hearken, ye people, from far; The Lord hath called me from the womb; from the bowels of my mother hath he made mention of my name. 2 And he hath made my mouth like a sharp sword; in the shadow of his hand hath he hid me, and made me a polished shaft; in his quiver hath he hid me; 3 And said unto me, Thou art my servant, O Israel, in whom I will be glorified. 4 Then I said, I have laboured in vain, I have spent my strength for nought, and in vain: yet surely my judgment is with the Lord, and my work with my God. 5 And now, saith the Lord that formed me from the womb to be his servant, to bring Jacob again to him, Though Israel be not gathered, yet shall I be glorious in the eyes of the Lord, and my God shall be my strength. 6 And he said, It is a light thing that thou shouldest be my servant to raise up the tribes of Jacob, and to restore the preserved of Israel: I will also give thee for a light to the Gentiles, that thou mayest be my salvation unto the end of the earth.

49.1-6 Thou art my servant speaking of the Messiah, formed… from the womb to be his servant and to bring Jacob again to him. He is the light to the Gentiles (Isa

11:10; 42:6-7, Acts 13:47) is fulfilled in Jesus. Salvation only comes through the death, burial and resurrection of Jesus Christ (Acts 2:38; 4:12; John 3:1-7)

49.7 Thus saith the Lord, the Redeemer of Israel, and his Holy One, to him whom man despiseth, to him whom the nation abhorreth, to a servant of rulers, Kings shall see and arise, princes also shall worship, because of the Lord that is faithful, and the Holy One of Israel, and he shall choose thee.

49.7 There is only one redeemer of Israel, he is the Holy One; who is despised (Ps 22:6; Isa 53:1-6), whom the nation abhorreth, all speaking of how Jesus came unto his own, and his own received him not. (John 1:10-11)

49.8-12 Thus saith the Lord, In an acceptable time have I heard thee, and in a day of salvation have I helped thee: and I will preserve thee, and give thee for a covenant of the people, to establish the earth, to cause to inherit the desolate heritages; 9 That thou mayest say to the prisoners, Go forth; to them that are in darkness, Shew yourselves. They shall feed in the ways, and their pastures shall be in all high places. 10 They shall not hunger nor thirst; neither shall the heat nor sun smite them: for he that hath mercy on them shall lead them, even by the springs of water shall he guide them. 11 And I will make all my mountains a way, and my highways shall be exalted. 12 Behold, these shall come from far: and, lo, these from the north and from the west; and these from the land of Sinim.

49.8-12 The reference to the covenant of the people, how that Christ became our high priest, the mediator of the New Testament (Heb 9:11-17)

49.13-26 Sing, O heavens; and be joyful, O earth; and break forth into singing, O mountains: for the Lord hath comforted his people, and will have mercy upon his afflicted. 14 But Zion said, The Lord hath forsaken me, and my Lord hath forgotten me. 15 Can a woman forget her sucking child, that she should not have compassion on the son of her womb? yea, they may forget, yet will I not forget thee. 16 Behold, I have graven thee upon the palms of my hands; thy walls are continually before me. 17 Thy children shall make haste; thy destroyers and they that made thee waste shall go forth of thee. 18 Lift up thine eyes round about, and behold: all these gather themselves together, and come to thee. As I live, saith the Lord, thou shalt surely clothe thee with them all, as with an ornament, and bind them on thee, as a bride doeth. 19 For thy waste and thy desolate places, and the land of thy destruction, shall even now be too narrow by reason of the inhabitants, and they that swallowed thee up shall be far away. 20 The children which thou shalt have, after thou hast lost the other, shall say again in thine ears, The place is too strait for me: give place to me that I may dwell. 21 Then shalt thou say in thine heart, Who hath begotten me these, seeing I have lost my children, and am desolate, a captive, and removing to and fro? and who hath brought up these? Behold, I was left alone; these, where had they been? 22 Thus saith the Lord God, Behold, I will lift up mine hand to the Gentiles, and set up my standard to the people: and they shall bring thy sons in their arms, and thy daughters shall be carried upon their shoulders. 23 And kings shall be thy nursing fathers, and their queens thy nursing mothers: they shall bow down to thee with their face toward the earth, and lick up the dust of thy feet; and thou shalt know that I am the Lord: for they shall not be ashamed that wait for me. 24 Shall the prey be taken from the mighty, or the lawful captive delivered? 25 But thus saith the Lord, Even the captives of the mighty shall be taken away, and the prey of the terrible shall be delivered: for I will contend with him that contendeth with thee, and I will save thy children. 26 And I will feed them that oppress thee with their own flesh; and they shall be drunken with their own blood, as with sweet wine: and all flesh shall know that I the Lord am thy Saviour and thy Redeemer, the mighty One of Jacob.

49.13-26 God reassures Israel that they are ever before Him, engraved [shaqaq, to "carve, cut, engrave"] upon the palms of his hands. Israel is the natural branch and the Gentiles are going to be engrafted in. (Rom 11:11-25; John 10:16) His new covenant with the Gentiles will bring both Jew and Gentile into one sheepfold.

Chapter 50

50.1-3 Thus saith the Lord, Where is the bill of your mother's divorcement, whom I have put away? or which of my creditors is it to whom I have sold you? Behold, for your iniquities have ye sold yourselves, and for your transgressions is your mother put away. 2 Wherefore, when I came, was there no man? when I called, was there none to answer? Is my hand shortened at all, that it cannot redeem? or have I no power to deliver? behold, at my rebuke I dry up the sea, I make the rivers a wilderness: their fish stinketh, because there is no water, and dieth for thirst. 3 I clothe the heavens with blackness, and I make sackcloth their covering.

50.1-3 God emphasizes His commitment of marriage to Israel, in spite of their backsliding. (Jer 3:8-14; Hosea 2:19-20)

50.4-11 The Lord God hath given me the tongue of the learned, that I should know how to speak a word in season to him that is weary: he wakeneth morning by morning, he wakeneth mine ear to hear as the learned. 5 The Lord God hath opened mine ear, and I was not rebellious, neither turned away back. 6 I gave my back

to the smiters, and my cheeks to them that plucked off the hair: I hid not my face from shame and spitting. 7 For the Lord God will help me; therefore shall I not be confounded: therefore have I set my face like a flint, and I know that I shall not be ashamed. 8 He is near that justifieth me; who will contend with me? let us stand together: who is mine adversary? let him come near to me. 9 Behold, the Lord God will help me; who is he that shall condemn me? lo, they all shall wax old as a garment; the moth shall eat them up. 10 Who is among you that feareth the Lord, that obeyeth the voice of his servant, that walketh in darkness, and hath no light? let him trust in the name of the Lord, and stay upon his God. 11 Behold, all ye that kindle a fire, that compass yourselves about with sparks: walk in the light of your fire, and in the sparks that ye have kindled. This shall ye have of mine hand; ye shall lie down in sorrow.

50.4-11 Messiah will have the tongue of the learned, as Jesus exemplified, speaking with authority and wisdom that left men astonished. (Mat 7:28-29; 13:54) Christ's suffering is shown here with giving his back to the smiters, plucking his beard and being spit upon. (Isa 52:14; Matt 26:67, 27:30; Mark 14:65; Luke 18:32) He who knew no sin was made sin for us. (2 Cor 5:19-21; 1 Pet 3:18)

Chapter 51

51.1-16 Hearken to me, ye that follow after righteousness, ye that seek the Lord: look unto the rock whence ye are hewn, and to the hole of the pit whence ye are digged. 2 Look unto Abraham your father, and unto Sarah that bare you: for I called him alone, and blessed him, and increased him. 3 For the Lord shall comfort Zion: he will comfort all her waste places; and he will make her wilderness like Eden, and her desert like the garden of the Lord; joy and gladness shall be found therein, thanksgiving, and the voice of melody. 4 Hearken unto me, my people; and give ear unto me, O my nation: for a law shall proceed from me, and I will make my judgment to rest for a light of the people. 5 My righteousness is near; my salvation is gone forth, and mine arms shall judge the people; the isles shall wait upon me, and on mine arm shall they trust. 6 Lift up your eyes to the heavens, and look upon the earth beneath: for the heavens shall vanish away like smoke, and the earth shall wax old like a garment, and they that dwell therein shall die in like manner: but my salvation shall be for ever, and my righteousness shall not be abolished. 7 Hearken unto me, ye that know righteousness, the people in whose heart is my law; fear ye not the reproach of men, neither be ye afraid of their revilings. 8 For the moth shall eat them up like a garment, and the worm shall eat them like wool: but my righteousness shall be for ever, and my salvation from generation to generation. 9 Awake, awake, put on strength, O arm of the Lord; awake, as in the ancient days, in the generations of old. Art thou not it that hath cut Rahab, and wounded the dragon? 10 Art thou not it which hath dried the sea, the waters of the great deep; that hath made the depths of the sea a way for the ransomed to pass over? 11 Therefore the redeemed of the Lord shall return, and come with singing unto Zion; and everlasting joy shall be upon their head: they shall obtain gladness and joy; and sorrow and mourning shall flee away. 12 I, even I, am he that comforteth you: who art thou, that thou shouldest be afraid of a man that shall die, and of the son of man which shall be made as grass; 13 And forgettest the Lord thy maker, that hath stretched forth the heavens, and laid the foundations of the earth; and hast feared continually every day because of the fury of the oppressor, as if he were ready to destroy? and where is the fury of the oppressor? 14 The captive exile hasteneth that he may be loosed, and that he should not die in the pit, nor that his bread should fail. 15 But I am the Lord thy God, that divided the sea, whose waves roared: The Lord of hosts is his name. 16 And I have put my words in thy mouth, and I have covered thee in the shadow of mine hand, that I may plant the heavens, and lay the foundations of the earth, and say unto Zion, Thou art my people.

51.1-16 Isaiah addresses three times with Hearken unto me, to the faithful portion of people that follow after righteousness. He sees the time where the Heavens shall vanish away and the earth will wax old like a garment. Jesus spoke of Heaven and earth passing away, but his words shall never pass away. Peter and John both foretold of it. (Matt 24:35; 2 Pet 3:10-13; Rev 21:1) Yet the redeemed of the Lord shall come with singing, everlasting joy and gladness.

51.17-23 Awake, awake, stand up, O Jerusalem, which hast drunk at the hand of the Lord the cup of his fury; thou hast drunken the dregs of the cup of trembling, and wrung them out. 18 There is none to guide her among all the sons whom she hath brought forth; neither is there any that taketh her by the hand of all the sons that she hath brought up. 19 These two things are come unto thee; who shall be sorry for thee? desolation, and destruction, and the famine, and the sword: by whom shall I comfort thee? 20 Thy sons have fainted, they lie at the head of all the streets, as a wild bull in a net: they are full of the fury of the Lord, the rebuke of thy God. 21 Therefore hear now this, thou afflicted, and drunken, but not with wine: 22 Thus saith thy Lord the Lord, and thy God that pleadeth the cause of his people, Behold, I have taken out of thine hand the cup of trembling, even the dregs of the cup of my fury; thou shalt no more drink it again: 23 But I will put it into the hand of them that afflict thee; which have said to thy soul, Bow down, that we may go over: and thou hast laid thy body as the ground, and as the street, to them that went over.

51.17-23 The cup of God's fury and rebuke was poured out on Jerusalem by Nebuchadnezzar (2 Kings 25:9-10)

Chapter 52

52.1-6 Awake, awake; put on thy strength, O Zion; put on thy beautiful garments, O Jerusalem, the holy city: for henceforth there shall no more come into thee the uncircumcised and the unclean. 2 Shake thyself from the dust; arise, and sit down, O Jerusalem: loose thyself from the bands of thy neck, O captive daughter of Zion. 3 For thus saith the Lord, Ye have sold yourselves for nought; and ye shall be redeemed without money. 4 For thus saith the Lord God, My people went down aforetime into Egypt to sojourn there; and the Assyrian oppressed them without cause. 5 Now therefore, what have I here, saith the Lord, that my people is taken away for nought? they that rule over them make them to howl, saith the Lord; and my name continually every day is blasphemed. 6 Therefore my people shall know my name: therefore they shall know in that day that I am he that doth speak: behold, it is I.

52.1-6 Isaiah continues his third plea for Jerusalem to awake. Reminding them that they shall be redeemed and know His name.

52.7-12 How beautiful upon the mountains are

the feet of him that bringeth good tidings, that publisheth peace; that bringeth good tidings of good, that publisheth salvation; that saith unto Zion, Thy God reigneth! 8 Thy watchmen shall lift up the voice; with the voice together shall they sing: for they shall see eye to eye, when the Lord shall bring again Zion. 9 Break forth into joy, sing together, ye waste places of Jerusalem: for the Lord hath comforted his people, he hath redeemed Jerusalem. 10 The Lord hath made bare his holy arm in the eyes of all the nations; and all the ends of the earth shall see the salvation of our God. 11 Depart ye, depart ye, go ye out from thence, touch no unclean thing; go ye out of the midst of her; be ye clean, that bear the vessels of the Lord. 12 For ye shall not go out with haste, nor go by flight: for the Lord will go before you; and the God of Israel will be your reward.

52.7-12 Paul quotes from this passage; How beautiful upon the mountains are the feet of him that bringeth good tidings, that publisheth peace regarding the preaching of the gospel Rom 10:14-15. To bring good tidings (mebaser) means to "preach" or "carry good news."

52.13-15 Behold, my servant shall deal prudently, he shall be exalted and extolled, and be very high. 14 As many were astonied at thee; his visage was so marred more than any man, and his form more than the sons of men: 15 So shall he sprinkle many nations; the kings shall shut their mouths at him: for that which had not been told them shall they see; and that which they had not heard shall they consider.

52.13-15 Isaiah begins here and throughout chapter

53 to reveal the servant of the Lord identified as the Messiah who suffers for our sins. The terms exalted and extolled, and be very high are used only in (Isa 33:10 and here, but nowhere else in the prophets. Jesus Christ is the Messiah shown here Mt 8:17; Mk 15:28; Lk 22:37; Jn 12:38; Acts 8:28-35; Rom 10:16; 1 Pe 2:21-25. His visage was marred, Castalio translates, "so that is was no longer that of a man." Jesus was born of a virgin (Isa 7:14; Mt 1:23) from the linage of David (11:1).

Chapter 53

53.1-2 Who hath believed our report? and to whom is the arm of the Lord revealed? 2 For he shall grow up before him as a tender plant, and as a root out of a dry ground: he hath no form nor comeliness; and when we shall see him, there is no beauty that we should desire him.

53.1-2 Continuing his description of Messiah, God manifest in the flesh, Jesus Christ the Son of God, not God the Son, who was given for the atonement of our sins. Jesus is the root and the offspring of David (Isa 11:1, 10; Rev 5:5) Isaiah 9:6 declares a child is born, a son is given: his name shall be called Wonderful, Counsellor, The mighty God, The everlasting Father, The Prince of Peace. Here we see the manifestation of God in Christ. A son is given, who is the Everlasting Father. Jesus declared I and my Father are one. (Jn 10:30; 1 Tim 3:16; 2 Cor 5:19)

53.3-5 He is despised and rejected of men; a man of sorrows, and acquainted with grief: and we hid as it were our faces from him; he was despised, and we esteemed him not. 4 Surely he hath borne our griefs, and carried our sorrows: yet we did esteem

him stricken, smitten of God, and afflicted. 5 But he was wounded for our transgressions, he was bruised for our iniquities: the chastisement of our peace was upon him; and with his stripes we are healed.**

53.3-5 Despised (from bazah, "to disdain or scorn") (Is 49:7; Ps 22:6) and rejected [shadal, "abandoned"] of men (Jn 6:66; Mt 26:56), a man of sorrows (mak'obot, severe pains) and acquainted with grief (choli, "injuries"). He hath borne our griefs (lit., "spiritual sickness") (Mt 20:28; Jn 11:50-52; Ro 3:25; 5:6-8; 8:3; 2 Co 5:18-21; 8:9; Gal 3:13; Ep 1:7; 1 Pe 2:24) he carried our sorrows (Mt 8:17). All of this was fulfilled in Christ's suffering (Mt 27:39-44) But he was wounded [or "pierced through"] for our transgressions (sins), by the thorns, the nails, and by the soldiers spear. He was bruised daka', meaning "to be utterly crushed." Our iniquities ('awon) means moral "evils,". . Chastisement [musar, "correction" or "discipline"] of our peace refers to that which procured our peace with God (Ep 2:15-17; Col 1:20). With his stripes (or "wounds"), speaking of Jesus being scourged (Mt 27:26) we are healed (rapa, to mend or cure). 1 Peter 2:21-24 connects our healing to the stripes Jesus received in his body for us.

53.6-9 All we like sheep have gone astray; we have turned every one to his own way; and the Lord hath laid on him the iniquity of us all. 7 He was oppressed, and he was afflicted, yet he opened not his mouth: he is brought as a lamb to the slaughter, and as a sheep before her shearers is dumb, so he openeth not his mouth. 8 He was taken from prison and from judgment: and who shall declare his generation? for he was cut off out of the land of the living: for the transgression of my people was he stricken. 9 And he made his grave with the wicked, and with the rich in his death; because he had done no violence, neither was any deceit in his mouth.

53.6-9 We are like the sheep gone astray (Ps 119:176). The Lord hath laid on him the iniquity of us all. The sinless Lamb became our sacrifice (Mt 26:39; 1 Jn 4:10; 2 Co 5:21). He opened not His mouth is illustrated by a lamb being brought to the slaughter. (John 1:29; Rev 5:6, 12). In Acts 8:27-39 a man from Ethiopia, read from this portion of Isaiah, asking whom this spoke of. Philip began at the same scripture and preached Jesus to him, explaining the death, burial and resurrection of Christ. After understanding this we see him being baptized in Jesus name. Jesus was crucified between two thieves making his grave with the wicked (Mt 27:38). And with the rich in his death refers to Jesus' burial in the tomb of the wealthy Joseph of Arimathea (Matt 27:57)

53.10-12 Yet it pleased the Lord to bruise him; he hath put him to grief: when thou shalt make his soul an offering for sin, he shall see his seed, he shall prolong his days, and the pleasure of the Lord shall prosper in his hand. 11 He shall see of the travail of his soul, and shall be satisfied: by his knowledge shall my righteous servant justify many; for he shall bear their iniquities. 12 Therefore will I divide him a portion with the great, and he shall divide the spoil with the strong; because he hath poured out his soul unto death: and he was numbered with the transgressors; and he bare the sin of many, and made intercession for the transgressors.

53.10-12 It pleased the LORD to bruise [from daka', "to crush"] Him also prophetically fulfills (Gen 3:15)

An offering for sin (asham, "guilt offering") Neither by the blood of bulls and calves, but by his own blood he entered in once into the holy place, having obtained eternal redemption for us... without the shedding of blood there is no remission for sins. (Heb 7:26-27; 9:11-14, 20-28; 10:1-18' 1 Pet 1:18-21) We are redeemed with the precious blood of Christ, as of a lamb without blemish and without spot. This blood is applied when we are baptized in the name of Jesus Christ for the remission of sins. (Acts 2:37-39; 10:44-48; 19:1-6; 22:16). His intercession refers to His high priestly ministry, by which He makes intercession on the basis of His own substitutionary death.

Chapter 54

54.1-17 Sing, O barren, thou that didst not bear; break forth into singing, and cry aloud, thou that didst not travail with child: for more are the children of the desolate than the children of the married wife, saith the Lord. 2 Enlarge the place of thy tent, and let them stretch forth the curtains of thine habitations: spare not, lengthen thy cords, and strengthen thy stakes; 3 For thou shalt break forth on the right hand and on the left; and thy seed shall inherit the Gentiles, and make the desolate cities to be inhabited. 4 Fear not; for thou shalt not be ashamed: neither be thou confounded; for thou shalt not be put to shame: for thou shalt forget the shame of thy youth, and shalt not remember the reproach of thy widowhood any more. 5 For thy Maker is thine husband; the Lord of hosts is his name; and thy Redeemer the Holy One of Israel; The God of the whole earth shall he be called. 6 For the Lord hath called thee as a woman forsaken and grieved in spirit, and a wife of youth, when thou wast refused, saith thy God. 7 For a small moment have I forsaken thee; but with great mercies will I gather thee. 8 In a little wrath I hid my face from thee for a moment; but with everlasting kindness will I have mercy on thee, saith the Lord thy Redeemer. 9 For this is as the waters of Noah unto me:

for as I have sworn that the waters of Noah should no more go over the earth; so have I sworn that I would not be wroth with thee, nor rebuke thee. 10 For the mountains shall depart, and the hills be removed; but my kindness shall not depart from thee, neither shall the covenant of my peace be removed, saith the Lord that hath mercy on thee. 11 O thou afflicted, tossed with tempest, and not comforted, behold, I will lay thy stones with fair colours, and lay thy foundations with sapphires. 12 And I will make thy windows of agates, and thy gates of carbuncles, and all thy borders of pleasant stones. 13 And all thy children shall be taught of the Lord; and great shall be the peace of thy children. 14 In righteousness shalt thou be established: thou shalt be far from oppression; for thou shalt not fear: and from terror; for it shall not come near thee. 15 Behold, they shall surely gather together, but not by me: whosoever shall gather together against thee shall fall for thy sake. 16 Behold, I have created the smith that bloweth the coals in the fire, and that bringeth forth an instrument for his work; and I have created the waster to destroy. 17 No weapon that is formed against thee shall prosper; and every tongue that shall rise against thee in judgment thou shalt condemn. This is the heritage of the servants of the Lord, and their righteousness is of me, saith the Lord.

54:1-17 God's promise to Israel barren womb is that she shall break forth abundantly for the Lord is her husband. God reminds her yet again his mercies are hers and his kindness and peace will never leave her. How great is Gods faithfulness to His people. Even in the midst of all the enemy comes against us with, nothing shall prosper against His church. Jesus said the gates of hell shall not prevail against the church. (Mt 16:18)

Chapter 55

55.1-5 Ho, every one that thirsteth, come ye to the waters, and he that hath no money; come ye, buy, and eat; yea, come, buy wine and milk without money and without price. 2 Wherefore do ye spend money for that which is not bread? and your labour for that which satisfieth not? hearken diligently unto me, and eat ye that which is good, and let your soul delight itself in fatness. 3 Incline your ear, and come unto me: hear, and your soul shall live; and I will make an everlasting covenant with you, even the sure mercies of David. 4 Behold, I have given him for a witness to the people, a leader and commander to the people. 5 Behold, thou shalt call a nation that thou knowest not, and nations that knew not thee shall run unto thee because of the Lord thy God, and for the Holy One of Israel; for he hath glorified thee.

55.1-5 Every one that thirsteth, Jesus cried, "If any man thirst, let him come unto me and drink. He that believeth on me as the scriptures have said, out of his belly shall flow rivers of living water." He spoke of the Spirit, which they that believe on him should receive: for the Holy Ghost was not yet given, because Jesus was not yet glorified. This was fulfilled on the day of Pentecost in Acts 2:1-4 when the Holy Ghost was poured out in the upper room. Around 120 people were gloriously filled and spoke with other tongues as the Spirit gave them the utterance. This is the gift that every believer should receive as a part of the new birth.

55.6-13 Seek ye the Lord while he may be found, call ye upon him while he is near: 7 Let the wicked forsake his way, and the unrighteous man his thoughts: and let him return unto the Lord, and he will have mercy upon him; and to our God, for he will abundantly pardon. 8 For my thoughts are not your thoughts, neither are your ways my ways, saith the Lord. 9 For as the heavens are higher than the earth, so are my ways higher than your ways, and my thoughts than your thoughts. 10 For as the rain cometh down, and the snow from heaven, and returneth not thither, but watereth the earth, and maketh it bring forth and bud, that it may give seed to the sower, and bread to the eater: 11 So shall my word be that goeth forth out of my mouth: it shall not return unto me void, but it shall accomplish that which I please, and it shall prosper in the thing whereto I sent it. 12 For ye shall go out with joy, and be led forth with peace: the mountains and the hills shall break forth before you into singing, and all the trees of the field shall clap their hands. 13 Instead of the thorn shall come up the fir tree, and instead of the brier shall come up the myrtle tree: and it shall be to the Lord for a name, for an everlasting sign that shall not be cut off.

55.6-13 God calls us to seek Him while he may be found and call on him when he is near. For God is a rewarder of those who will diligently seek Him (Heb 11:6) Importance is to seek him with your whole heart.

Seeking after God will not benefit the seeker unless there is a genuine act of repentance. Repentance is forsaking wickedness and unrighteous thoughts, turning to God who will have mercy and abundantly pardon. God's ways and thoughts are so much higher than ours. The power of Gods word carries with it the promise of growth and change. Never forget that Heaven and Earth shall pass away, but His word shall never pass away. IT will never return void, but always accomplishes His purposes. (2 Cor 1:20)

Chapter 56

56.1-12 Thus saith the Lord, Keep ye judgment, and do justice: for my salvation is near to come, and my righteousness to be revealed. 2 Blessed is the man that doeth this, and the son of man that layeth hold on it; that keepeth the sabbath from polluting it, and keepeth his hand from doing any evil. 3 Neither let the son of the stranger, that hath joined himself to the Lord, speak, saying, The Lord hath utterly separated me from his people: neither let the eunuch say, Behold, I am a dry tree. 4 For thus saith the Lord unto the eunuchs that keep my sabbaths, and choose the things that please me, and take hold of my covenant; 5 Even unto them will I give in mine house and within my walls a place and a name better than of sons and of daughters: I will give them an everlasting name, that shall not be cut off. 6 Also the sons of the stranger, that join themselves to the Lord, to serve him, and to love the name of the Lord, to be his servants, every one that keepeth the sabbath from polluting it, and taketh hold of my covenant; 7 Even them will I bring to my holy mountain, and make them joyful in my house of prayer: their burnt offerings and their sacrifices shall be accepted upon mine altar; for mine house shall be called an house of prayer for all people. 8

The Lord God, which gathereth the outcasts of Israel saith, Yet will I gather others to him, beside those that are gathered unto him. 9 All ye beasts of the field, come to devour, yea, all ye beasts in the forest. 10 His watchmen are blind: they are all ignorant, they are all dumb dogs, they cannot bark; sleeping, lying down, loving to slumber. 11 Yea, they are greedy dogs which can never have enough, and they are shepherds that cannot understand: they all look to their own way, every one for his gain, from his quarter. 12 Come ye, say they, I will fetch wine, and we will fill ourselves with strong drink; and to morrow shall be as this day, and much more abundant.

56.1-12 Blessings are upon the obedient that turn from doing evil. To the eunuch and the stranger, both can through repentance and loving God, take hold of his covenant…for mine house shall be called an house of prayer for all people, (1 Kings 8:29-53) Jesus quoted from this passage and cleansed the temple, bringing the purpose of prayer back to the house of God, for both Jew and Gentile. (Ps 141:2; 51:17; Mal 1:11 Mat 21:13) The chapter ends with an indictment of the watchmen (or prophets) who are blind… ignorant… dumb dogs.

Chapter 57

57.1 The righteous perisheth, and no man layeth it to heart: and merciful men are taken away, none considering that the righteous is taken away from the evil to come.

57.1 The Holy One perishes, but no one will care. (*A prophet is without honor in His own country*, Matt. 13:57). More immediately, those living virtuous lives often die before their time, but are spared more evil days and judgment to come.

57.2 He shall enter into peace: they shall rest in their beds, each one walking in his uprightness.

57.2 The ones that die in a pure heart are granted the peace of eternal rest.

57.3-4 But draw near hither, ye sons of the sorceress, the seed of the adulterer and the whore. 4 Against whom do ye sport yourselves? against whom make ye a wide mouth, and draw out the tongue? are ye not children of transgression, a seed of falsehood.

57.3-4 How is it that the wicked think to mock the

righteous, seeing that they are sons and daughters of immorality, deserving of scorn themselves?

57.5-7 Enflaming yourselves with idols under every green tree, slaying the children in the valleys under the clifts of the rocks? 6 Among the smooth stones of the stream is thy portion; they, they are thy lot: even to them hast thou poured a drink offering, thou hast offered a meat offering. Should I receive comfort in these? 7 Upon a lofty and high mountain hast thou set thy bed: even thither wentest thou up to offer sacrifice.

57.5-7 The debased commit idolatry everywhere they can; they offer their very children as sacrifices. The libation stones have become their gods. The LORD is hotly displeased; every available mountaintop has become a heathen high place.

57.8 Behind the doors also and the posts hast thou set up thy remembrance: for thou hast discovered thyself to another than me, and art gone up; thou hast enlarged thy bed, and made thee a covenant with them; thou lovedst their bed where thou sawest it.

57.8 Their homes are adorned with the symbols and unclothed statues of idols.

57.9 And thou wentest to the king with ointment, and didst increase thy perfumes, and didst send thy messengers far off, and didst debase thyself even unto hell.

57.9 The vile Molech has been anointed with oil and sweet perfume; the idolators have gone to great lengths to find new gods, straying so far as to necromancy. (Or, *king* {Molech} may be indicative of the alliances Israel attempted to forge with Godless nations rather than turn to the Lord for deliverance.)

57.10 Thou art wearied in the greatness of thy way; yet saidst thou not, There is no hope: thou hast found the life of thine hand; therefore thou wast not grieved.

57.10 The search for help, peace, or purpose in any other but the One God can end only weariness. The constant pursuit of the "pleasures of sin for a season" (Heb. 11:25) never satisfies and therefore never ends.

57.11-12 And of whom hast thou been afraid or feared, that thou hast lied, and hast not remembered me, nor laid it to thy heart? have not I held my peace even of old, and thou fearest me not? 12 I will declare thy righteousness, and thy works; for they shall not profit thee.

57.11-12 What substitute could impose more awe than the Word of God? What idol could cause one to no longer fear the Judgment of Mighty God? All alleged uprightness of man, his spurious deviation to *come up some other way* (John 10:1), will be exposed for the fraud it is. (Man is easily swayed to another gospel, *which is not another* Gal. 1:6-7)

57.13-15 When thou criest, let thy companies deliver thee; but the wind shall carry them all away; vanity shall take them: but he that putteth his trust in me shall possess the land, and shall inherit my holy mountain; 14 And shall say, Cast ye up, cast ye up, prepare the way, take up the stumblingblock out of the way of my people. 15 For thus saith the high and lofty One

that inhabiteth eternity, whose name is Holy; I dwell in the high and holy place, with him also that is of a contrite and humble spirit, to revive the spirit of the humble, and to revive the heart of the contrite ones.

57.13-15 Can the idols of man save him in time of trouble? They are worthless. The Lord will prepare the way for those that trust in Him. He will restore the heart full of humility, of contrition the one who will obey. (Ps. 51:17, 1 Sam. 15:22)

57.16-19 For I will not contend for ever, neither will I be always wroth: for the spirit should fail before me, and the souls which I have made. 17 For the iniquity of his covetousness was I wroth, and smote him: I hid me, and was wroth, and he went on frowardly in the way of his heart. 18 I have seen his ways, and will heal him: I will lead him also, and restore comforts unto him and to his mourners. 19 I create the fruit of the lips; Peace, peace to him that is far off, and to him that is near, saith the Lord; and I will heal him.

57.16-19 Though disobedience brings judgment, the Lord is merciful and will not remain angry forever, lest all mankind be destroyed for good. (Jer. 4:27) There is hope still that praise might be found on the lips of the broken. (Job 14:7)

57.20-21 But the wicked are like the troubled sea, when it cannot rest, whose waters cast up mire and dirt. 21 There is no peace, saith my God, to the wicked.

57. 20-21 However, for the one who chooses wickedness continually in the face of undeserved mercy, there shall be no peace. (Isaiah reminds us of the Law set down in

Lev. 26; the Lord desires reconciliation, but those who walk contrary, those who will not be reformed, will be chastised.)

Chapter 58

58.1 Cry aloud, spare not, lift up thy voice like a trumpet, and shew my people their transgression, and the house of Jacob their sins.

58.1 The trespass of God's people must not be kept secret. (1 Tim. 5:20)

58.2-5 Yet they seek me daily, and delight to know my ways, as a nation that did righteousness, and forsook not the ordinance of their God: they ask of me the ordinances of justice; they take delight in approaching to God. 3 Wherefore have we fasted, say they, and thou seest not? wherefore have we afflicted our soul, and thou takest no knowledge? Behold, in the day of your fast ye find pleasure, and exact all your labours. 4 Behold, ye fast for strife and debate, and to smite with the fist of wickedness: ye shall not fast as ye do this day, to make your voice to be heard on high. 5 Is it such a fast that I have chosen? a day for a man to afflict his soul? is it to bow down his head as a bulrush, and to spread sackcloth and ashes under him? wilt thou call this a fast, and an acceptable day to the Lord?

58.2-5 Traditional religious rites, rote memorization,

and ecclesiastical ritual are not enough to make one spiritual or pleasing to God. It was for such unbalanced hypocrisy that the Lord condemned the pharisees. (Matt. 23:23) The Lord will not tolerate the vestigial appearance of Godliness while concurrently "denying the power thereof." (2 Tim. 3:5)

58.6-7 Is not this the fast that I have chosen? to loose the bands of wickedness, to undo the heavy burdens, and to let the oppressed go free, and that ye break every yoke? 7 Is it not to deal thy bread to the hungry, and that thou bring the poor that are cast out to thy house? when thou seest the naked, that thou cover him; and that thou hide not thyself from thine own flesh?

58.6-7 God's ideal fast requires more than fleshly eschewing of food. Moreover, He desires an ancillary abstinence from partaking in unrighteous action. The Lord is eager for His people to yearn for principled, law-abiding, virtuous conduct. His thought and view of fasting is far above our own. (Is. 55:9)

58.8-9 Then shall thy light break forth as the morning, and thine health shall spring forth speedily: and thy righteousness shall go before thee; the glory of the Lord shall be thy reward. 9 Then shalt thou call, and the Lord shall answer; thou shalt cry, and he shall say, Here I am. If thou take away from the midst of thee the yoke, the putting forth of the finger, and speaking vanity;

58.8-9 A righteously motivated walk in Him guarantees spiritual victory; He will provide protection with His rear guard. When His people cease from vain iniquity,

His answer to our cry will be a resounding "Yes." (2 Chron. 7:14)

58.10-12 And if thou draw out thy soul to the hungry, and satisfy the afflicted soul; then shall thy light rise in obscurity, and thy darkness be as the noon day: 11 And the Lord shall guide thee continually, and satisfy thy soul in drought, and make fat thy bones: and thou shalt be like a watered garden, and like a spring of water, whose waters fail not. 12 And they that shall be of thee shall build the old waste places: thou shalt raise up the foundations of many generations; and thou shalt be called, The repairer of the breach, The restorer of paths to dwell in.

58.10-12 If the needy are provided for, the Law is satisfied, the Lord will "bless thee in all the work of thine hand…" (Lev. 22:13, Deut 10:18, Deut. 14:29), and He will devise means to help restore the city that was broken down. (Jer. 30:18, 2. Sam 14:14)

58.13-14. If thou turn away thy foot from the sabbath, from doing thy pleasure on my holy day; and call the sabbath a delight, the holy of the Lord, honourable; and shalt honour him, not doing thine own ways, nor finding thine own pleasure, nor speaking thine own words: 14 Then shalt thou delight thyself in the Lord; and I will cause thee to ride upon the high places of the earth, and feed thee with the heritage of Jacob thy father: for the mouth of the Lord hath spoken it.

58.13-14 Keep the Sabbath day Holy (Ex. 20:8), maintain its sacredness with a glad heart. When our "delight is in the law of the Lord" (Ps. 1:2) we become heirs to the promises of Jacob.

Chapter 59

59.1-2 Behold, the Lord's hand is not shortened, that it cannot save; neither his ear heavy, that it cannot hear: 2 But your iniquities have separated between you and your God, and your sins have hid his face from you, that he will not hear.

59.1-2 The arm and the ear are a metonymy for the Lord's unlimited saving power and His ever-listening acknowledgment of the prayerful cry. It is not God's inability that has prevented a liberation, but the sin of the people has severed the life-sustaining rescue line.

59.3-4 For your hands are defiled with blood, and your fingers with iniquity; your lips have spoken lies, your tongue hath muttered perverseness. 4 None calleth for justice, nor any pleadeth for truth: they trust in vanity, and speak lies; they conceive mischief, and bring forth iniquity.

59.3-4 Murderous schemes, wicked immorality, deception, and filthy conversation have become the social norm. The populace clamors for more impropriety over truth. (Col. 3:8; 2 Pet. 3:11)

59.5 They hatch cockatrice' eggs, and weave the spider's web: he that eateth of their eggs dieth, and that which is crushed breaketh out into a viper.

59.5 The egg of the cockatrice (*adder, basilisk, viper*) is the conception of falsehood that causes the poisoning of the soul. The Pharisees of Jesus' day were likewise compared to vipers, for if poison lies in the heart, it will be birthed from the lips (Matt. 12:34). Those who speak hypocrisy and falsehood weave a self-spun web of deceit.

59.6 Their webs shall not become garments, neither shall they cover themselves with their works: their works are works of iniquity, and the act of violence is in their hands.

59.6 Unlike the mulberry silkworm, the silk of spiders is not used to weave garments. The spider's web is spun for one purpose only, to catch its prey. But the web of self-righteousness, the contrivances of the self-justifying heart, though they may seize others in their clutches, cannot cover their own iniquity.

59.7-8 Their feet run to evil, and they make haste to shed innocent blood: their thoughts are thoughts of iniquity; wasting and destruction are in their paths. 8 The way of peace they know not; and there is no judgment in their goings: they have made them crooked paths: whosoever goeth therein shall not know peace.

59.7-8 These are the same hands and feet of Solomonic fame that God detests (Prov. 6:16-19). Their thoughts are not God's thoughts (Isa. 55:8-9). These are those who try and enter at the wide gate of destruction, a generation whose paths are untoward, not straight (Matt. 7:13-14; Acts 2:40).

59.9-11 Therefore is judgment far from us, neither doth justice overtake us: we wait for light, but behold obscurity; for brightness, but we walk in darkness. 10 We grope for the wall like the blind, and we grope as if we had no eyes: we stumble at noon day as in the night; we are in desolate places as dead men. 11 We roar all like bears, and mourn sore like doves: we look for judgment, but there is none; for salvation, but it is far off from us.

59.9-11 Those living outside of the Light of God's Law will find nothing but confusion as the payment of their blind groping, no different than the search of Job in the midst of his calamity (Job 23:8-9).

59.12-14 For our transgressions are multiplied before thee, and our sins testify against us: for our transgressions are with us; and as for our iniquities, we know them; 13 In transgressing and lying against the Lord, and departing away from our God, speaking oppression and revolt, conceiving and uttering from the heart words of falsehood. 14 And judgment is turned away backward, and justice standeth afar off: for truth is fallen in the street, and equity cannot enter.

59.12-14 The blood-guiltiness of sin cries out from the Earth (Gen. 4:10) and bears witness against God's people. Truth is not allowed to stand in the streets, sincerity has been banned from the eternal courtroom.

59.15-17 Yea, truth faileth; and he that departeth from

evil maketh himself a prey: and the Lord saw it, and it displeased him that there was no judgment. 16 And he saw that there was no man, and wondered that there was no intercessor: therefore his arm brought salvation unto him; and his righteousness, it sustained him. 17 For he put on righteousness as a breastplate, and an helmet of salvation upon his head; and he put on the garments of vengeance for clothing, and was clad with zeal as a cloak.

59.15-17 The LORD is angered that there is none righteous to stand in the breach; He alone can succeed (Rev. 5:4-5). This is a Messianic prophecy. The arm, again, is a metonymy for the seat of power of and authority (Psalm 98:1). He was manifest in flesh (1 Tim. 3:16). Clad in His own armor (Eph. 6:14-17) He brought salvation to Himself.

59.18 According to their deeds, accordingly he will repay, fury to his adversaries, recompence to his enemies; to the islands he will repay recompence.

59.18 He will take vengeance on His adversaries; according to their violation He will make retribution, every man rewarded according to His deeds (Matt. 16:27).

59.19 So shall they fear the name of the Lord from the west, and his glory from the rising of the sun. When the enemy shall come in like a flood, the Spirit of the Lord shall lift up a standard against him.

59.19 The East and West are metaphor; to the most extreme distance, to the ends of the Earth, every knee shall bow at the sound of His great name (Phil. 2:9-11).

The standard (*battle flag*, or *field sign*) was an ancient method of communication between friendly forces to aid in proper placement of troops and equipment on the battlefield. It would also serve as a warning sign aimed at scaring enemy forces into withdrawal or surrender. In this spiritual context, it is a. . formal notice of impending doom for all those who come against the Lord's holy purpose.

59.20-21 And the Redeemer shall come to Zion, and unto them that turn from transgression in Jacob, saith the Lord. 21 As for me, this is my covenant with them, saith the Lord; My spirit that is upon thee, and my words which I have put in thy mouth, shall not depart out of thy mouth, nor out of the mouth of thy seed, nor out of the mouth of thy seed's seed, saith the Lord, from henceforth and for ever.

59.20-21 This is further prophecy of the coming Christ (Rom. 11:26). Though the people may stray far, His covenant stands. So long as His Word is in their mouths, if His Word will not depart from their lips, the Redeemer will turn them from their transgressions. The Word did not depart, and His Word became flesh, and dwelt among us (John 1:1,14).

Chapter 60

60.1-3 Arise, shine; for thy light is come, and the glory of the Lord is risen upon thee. 2 For, behold, the darkness shall cover the earth, and gross darkness the people: but the Lord shall arise upon thee, and his glory shall be seen upon thee. 3 And the Gentiles shall come to thy light, and kings to the brightness of thy rising.

60.1-3 To *arise* is to be established, to stand up from servile imprisonment to sin. (Jer. 8:4) His people recover from a previously forlorn hopelessness. He has become light for His people and the eyes of both Israel and the Gentiles have seen salvation. (Isa. 49:6; Luke 2:25-32; Acts 13:47; Acts 26:23) Also, the arisen light and kings coming to the brightness of that rising, is perhaps prophecy of the Star of Bethlehem.

60.4 Lift up thine eyes round about, and see: all they gather themselves together, they come to thee: thy sons shall come from far, and thy daughters shall be nursed at thy side.

60.4 The diaspora will return from the ends of the Earth, Israel will be gathered to her promised land. (Jer. 30:3)

60.5-7 Then thou shalt see, and flow together, and thine heart shall fear, and be enlarged; because the abundance of the sea shall be converted unto thee, the forces of the Gentiles shall come unto thee. 6 The multitude of camels shall cover thee, the dromedaries of Midian and Ephah; all they from Sheba shall come: they shall bring gold and incense; and they shall shew forth the praises of the Lord. 7 All the flocks of Kedar shall be gathered together unto thee, the rams of Nebaioth shall minister unto thee: they shall come up with acceptance on mine altar, and I will glorify the house of my glory.

60.5-7 The collective force of God's Church is strengthened as the Gentiles see His light and come into His people. Glory, honor, and peace belong to all who work good is His Law; He shows no deference between peoples (Rom. 2:10-11). Midian, Ephah, Kedar, and Nabaioth are a metaphor for Gentile nations who will flock to His banner. Again, the mention of camels, Sheba, gold, and incense may be prophetic of the wise men's visit while following the Star out of Jacob (Num. 24:17).

60.8 Who are these that fly as a cloud, and as the doves to their windows?

60.8 Those rallying to the call of Israel in that day will be as a gathering cloud, as the bird of peace returning to its nesting place.

60.9-11 Surely the isles shall wait for me, and the ships of Tarshish first, to bring thy sons from far, their silver and their gold with them, unto the name of the Lord thy God, and to the Holy One of Israel, because he

hath glorified thee. 10 And the sons of strangers shall build up thy walls, and their kings shall minister unto thee: for in my wrath I smote thee, but in my favour have I had mercy on thee. 11 Therefore thy gates shall be open continually; they shall not be shut day nor night; that men may bring unto thee the forces of the Gentiles, and that their kings may be brought.

60.9-11 Tarshish, probably the island of Sardinia, was famed for its wealth and trade with Mediterranean nations, such as the with the Phoenicians and with Rome, as well as to the Middle East. (2 Chron. 9:21; Ps. 72:10; Jer. 10:9; Eze. 27:12,25). Its use here indicates the spoil that the Lord will deliver to Israel. The foreign ships and nations (*kings*) will serve (*minister*) to build Israel and return her people continually; even after disobedience, for the faithful heart His favor will not depart from His people.

60.12 For the nation and kingdom that will not serve thee shall perish; yea, those nations shall be utterly wasted.

60.12 Any nation that will not bow to Israel's dominion will be destroyed by Him.

60.13-14 The glory of Lebanon shall come unto thee, the fir tree, the pine tree, and the box together, to beautify the place of my sanctuary; and I will make the place of my feet glorious. 14 The sons also of them that afflicted thee shall come bending unto thee; and all they that despised thee shall bow themselves down at the soles of thy feet; and they shall call thee; The city of the Lord, The Zion of the Holy One of Israel.

60.13-14 It is the great cedars renowned of Solomon's era (1Kings 5:6,9), with the pines and cyprus too, that will once again build His great Temple. His dwelling place will no longer be an ark (Jer. 3:16-17) but His throne, His dwelling place, will be Jerusalem herself. The nations will bow at His footstool (Ps. 132:7) in Holy Zion, before the feet of the Lord when He comes into His Temple (Eze. 43:7; Mal. 3:1).

60.15-16 Whereas thou has been forsaken and hated, so that no man went through thee, I will make thee an eternal excellency, a joy of many generations. 16 Thou shalt also suck the milk of the Gentiles, and shalt suck the breast of kings: and thou shalt know that I the Lord am thy Saviour and thy Redeemer, the mighty One of Jacob.

60.15-16 Where once she lay in desolation (Isa. 34:10), abandoned, ignored, and ridiculed, Jerusalem will once again rise in grandeur (Ps. 47:4). All of Zion's needs will be provided (Isa. 49:23) by foreign nations that will give her milk (sustenance).

60.17-18 For brass I will bring gold, and for iron I will bring silver, and for wood brass, and for stones iron: I will also make thy officers peace, and thine exactors righteousness. 18 Violence shall no more be heard in thy land, wasting nor destruction within thy borders; but thou shalt call thy walls Salvation, and thy gates Praise.

60.17-18 This is the Heavenly exchange rate (Isa. 61:1-3). He provides better than what is deserved; He gives gladness for mourning (Ps. 30:5). He will remove sorrow, crying, and pain (Rev. 21:4), and gives unmerited Spiritual life in place of death.

60.19-20 The sun shall be no more thy light by day; neither for brightness shall the moon give light unto thee: but the Lord shall be unto thee an everlasting light, and thy God thy glory. 20 Thy sun shall no more go down; neither shall thy moon withdraw itself: for the Lord shall be thine everlasting light, and the days of thy mourning shall be ended.

60.19-20 Jesus Christ is the Light of the world (John 8:12). There will be no need for the heavenly bodies in that day (Zech. 14:6-7) for He will shine continuously. The sun and moon will be irrelevant and unnecessary; the Lamb of God is the Light of that Holy City (Rev. 21:23). There will be no more night; He will be Zion's fire and glory (Zech. 2:5; Rev. 22:5).

60.21-22 Thy people also shall be all righteous: they shall inherit the land for ever, the branch of my planting, the work of my hands, that I may be glorified. 22 A little one shall become a thousand, and a small one a strong nation: I the Lord will hasten it in his time.

60.21-22 Through this branch (*offshoot/descendent*) of Jesse (Isa. 11:1; Isa. 61:3; Jer. 23:5), the root of David (Rev. 5:5) will make righteous all those of His Church (Ps. 92:12-13; Rev. 21:27). The Lord takes the tiny mustard seed and brings a life-sustaining tree (Matt. 13:31-32); He will use the small and multiply it a thousand-fold (Micah 5:2) in His perfect time.

Chapter 61

61.1-2 The Spirit of the Lord God is upon me; because the Lord hath anointed me to preach good tidings unto the meek; he hath sent me to bind up the brokenhearted, to proclaim liberty to the captives, and the opening of the prison to them that are bound; 2 To proclaim the acceptable year of the Lord, and the day of vengeance of our God; to comfort all that mourn;

61.1-2 Many have contested whether or not Isaiah here speaks of himself or the Holy One. Indeed, much of the prophet's words embody a dual nature, bearing significance for both those oppressed Jews of his own age and import for all mankind through the coming Christ. However, the surrounding context, as well as the Lord's own reference to this passage, present an emphatic conclusion that this is Messianic prophecy. Approximately 700 years after these words were penned, the Lord Jesus enters the synagogue in Nazareth, the place of His upbringing, following 40 days of fasting and temptation in the wilderness. Upon opening the scroll of Isaiah, Jesus reads from this very passage and removes all doubt by proclaiming, *"This day is the scripture fulfilled in your ears,"* thus signaling that He is the One who will fulfill the words of the prophecy. (Luke 4:13-21)

61.3 To appoint unto them that mourn in Zion, to give unto them beauty for ashes, the oil of joy for mourning, the garment of praise for the spirit of heaviness; that they might be called trees of righteousness, the planting of the Lord, that he might be glorified.

61.3 Both immediately for the return of the Jews from exile, and eternally for the Church as a whole, the Lord will replace ashes with *beauty* ("a crown" or "garland"). Historically, during times of grief or mourning, the Jews would put on *sackcloth* ("a coarse fabric of flax, cotton, hemp, or goat/camel hair") and spread dust or ashes over their heads. Conversely, the *garment of praise* ("festive/royal attire") and jubilant anointing oil poured over the head demonstrated joy.

61.4-5 And they shall build the old wastes, they shall raise up the former desolations, and they shall repair the waste cities, the desolations of many generations. 5 And strangers shall stand and feed your flocks, and the sons of the alien shall be your plowmen and your vinedressers.

61.4-5 This may refer to the return from Babylonian captivity, but prophetically may have. pointed much further to Israel's diaspora, beginning in the 1st century AD and lasting almost two thousand years until the establishment of the Jewish state of Israel in 1948. The "*strangers feeding the flocks*" may be metaphors for the Gentiles taking the message of Jesus Christ to the Jews in the last days.

61.6 But ye shall be named the Priests of the Lord: men shall call you the Ministers of our God: ye shall eat the riches of the Gentiles, and in their glory shall ye boast yourselves.

61.6 It was only the priesthood that could perform the Holy Sacraments of Temple worship. It was only the High Priest who, but once a year, could enter the most Holy place. But the Lord has not left His people comfortless (John 14:18). With the indwelling of His Holy Ghost the bodies of His servants become the Temple (1 Cor. 6:19) and they the priests of His presence. (1 Pet. 2:5, 9; Rev. 1:6; Rev. 5:10)

61.7-9 For your shame ye shall have double; and for confusion they shall rejoice in their portion: therefore in their land they shall possess the double: everlasting joy shall be unto them. 8 For I the Lord love judgment, I hate robbery for burnt offering; and I will direct their work in truth, and I will make an everlasting covenant with them. 9 And their seed shall be known among the Gentiles, and their offspring among the people: all that see them shall acknowledge them, that they are the seed which the Lord hath blessed.

61.7-9 He is a rewarder of those that diligently seek Him (Heb. 11:6), those who endure persecution and difficulty to the end (Matthew 10:22). In that sojourn the Lord will have respect towards those who long for and abound in His law and justice (Amos 5:15; Luke 11:42; Phil. 1:9); He delights in those who desire the just weight (Prov. 11:1). He will never forget His everlasting covenant to the seed of Abraham (Gen. 12:2;17:7). The Church, born of Christ, are children of Abraham and made heirs to the promises. (Gal. 3:29)

61.10-11 I will greatly rejoice in the Lord, my soul shall be joyful in my God; for he hath clothed me with the garments of salvation, he hath covered me with the robe of righteousness, as a bridegroom decketh himself with ornaments, and as a bride adorneth herself with her jewels. 11 For as the earth bringeth forth her bud, and as the garden causeth the things that are sown in it to spring forth; so the Lord God will cause righteousness and praise to spring forth before all the nations.

61.10-11 The clothing of *"salvation"* is here the Hebrew *"yesha,"* or more literally, deliverance and freedom; in the joy of His Spirit we find that liberty from bondage to sin. (2. Cor. 3:17) The bride (the Church) and bridegroom (the Lord Himself) make themselves ready for that most wonderful celebratory union and beckon all to the marriage feast. (Rev. 22:17) Once the bleak winter of sin has past, the flowering spring of His glorious mercy arises in His perfect season.

Chapter 62

62.1 For Zion's sake will I not hold my peace, and for Jerusalem's sake I will not rest, until the righteousness thereof go forth as brightness, and the salvation thereof as a lamp that burneth.

62.1 First used in 2 Sam. 5:7, the word "*Zion*" referred to a mountain near Jerusalem, home to a Jebusite fortress conquered by David (renamed *The City of David*). Zion has since become representative of several aspects of the Judeo-Christian world, a symbol of the Temple, the eternal, holy city of Jerusalem herself, and "the church" as a whole. The prophet speaks that the LORD will never rest until Zion becomes the burning lamp of salvation to the world.

62.2 And the Gentiles shall see thy righteousness, and all kings thy glory: and thou shalt be called by a new name, which the mouth of the Lord shall name.

62.2 Where once Jerusalem, the church, had been mocked, scorned, and ridiculed, God will give a new name that will be recognized by all peoples and powers.

62.3-5 Thou shalt also be a crown of glory in the hand of

the Lord, and a royal diadem in the hand of thy God. 4 Thou shalt no more be termed Forsaken; neither shall thy land any more be termed Desolate: but thou shalt be called Hephzibah, and thy land Beulah: for the Lord delighteth in thee, and thy land shall be married. 5 For as a young man marrieth a virgin, so shall thy sons marry thee: and as the bridegroom rejoiceth over the bride, so shall thy God rejoice over thee.

62.3-5 The crown and diadem, those symbols of power and authority, will be placed upon Zion at the reunion of God and His people. When the LORD changes the name of a person or place, it denotes a transformation in character, a shift in purpose, an alternate future of events. The message of hope from the prophet lies in the fact that, once the nation of Israel turns from her idolatrous ways, she will no more be called "*Forsaken*" and. "*Desolate*" but will become "*Hephzibah*" (Hebrew: my delight is in her) and "*Beulah*" (Hebrew: married). This is the marriage referred to by the New Testament writers of Christ (the bridegroom) and His bride (the Church). (John 3:29; Eph. 5:22-33; Rev. 19:7; Rev. 21:2, 9-10)

62.6 I have set watchmen upon thy walls, O Jerusalem, which shall never hold their peace day nor night: ye that make mention of the Lord, keep not silence,

62.6 Historically, the watchmen would be those individuals placed in set, timed guard duties upon a city's defensive fortifications; their principle function was to serve as continual surveillance for enemy threats. In this setting Isaiah relays the message that the LORD has set watchmen over His people for their protection, not only from physical danger, but for the battle of their minds. As both Ezekiel and Hosea proclaimed, the Lord's prophets would serve to safeguard the people's interests by continually reminding them of the laws of God. (Eze. 3:17; 33:7; Hos. 9:8) Like the prophet Jeremiah, the Apostle Paul expanded this idea of the watchman into the role of pastors, as they "watch for your souls." (Jer. 3:12-15; Heb. 13:17)

62.7-9 And give him no rest, till he establish, and till he make Jerusalem a praise in the earth. 8 The Lord hath sworn by his right hand, and by the arm of his strength, Surely I will no more give thy corn to be meat for thine enemies; and the sons of the stranger shall not drink thy wine, for the which thou hast laboured: 9 But they that have gathered it shall eat it, and praise the Lord; and they that have brought it together shall drink it in the courts of my holiness.

62.7-9 The watchman of verse 6 is also, by extension, the Savior. Acting as a metonymy of the Messiah, the LORD swears by His own *"right hand"* and *"arm of His strength,"* the seat of power (Heb. 12:2; 1 Pet. 3:22; Rev. 1:17), for there is none greater to swear by. (Heb. 6:13; Rev. 1:17) The corn and grapes, the gain and harvest of God's people *"which was lost"* (Luke 19:10), will be won back and they will praise Him for His redemptive power. (Luke 1:68)

62.10-12 Go through, go through the gates; prepare ye the way of the people; cast up, cast up the highway; gather out the stones; lift up a standard for the people. 11 Behold, the Lord hath proclaimed unto the end of the world, Say ye to the daughter of Zion, Behold, thy salvation cometh; behold, his reward is with him, and his work before him. 12 And they shall call them, The

holy people, The redeemed of the Lord: and thou shalt be called, Sought out, A city not forsaken.

62.10-12 The LORD has opened wide the gates of the Holy City so that His people may come in. All obstacles have been removed; the LORD lifts up His standard against all who would oppose His children (Isa. 59:19). By His own salvation He has declared the saving of His people for the appointed end of time. (Matt. 13:40-49; 24:14; Heb. 9:26) They are no longer known by their former name, but have been given a new and glorious name, a people taken out for His namesake (Act 15:14), that the redeemed of the Lord may say so. (Ps. 107:2; Jer. 31:11; Lam. 3:58)

Chapter 63

63.1 Who is this that cometh from Edom, with dyed garments from Bozrah? this that is glorious in his apparel, travelling in the greatness of his strength? I that speak in righteousness, mighty to save.

63.1 In Biblical history the Edomites (descendants of Jacob's brother Esau) were a prominent and perpetual enemy of Israel. Edom refused to allow Israel to pass through their territory on the journey towards the Promised Land. King Saul battled with Edom, and David would go on to war with them and subjugate the nation for a time. Within a generation Edom was fighting with King Solomon. They resisted King Jehoshaphat, and they rose in rebellion against King Jehoram. When Greek later became the lingua franca of the region, the Edomites became known as the Idumeans. It comes as no surprise then that Herod the Great, that bloody king who thought to slay the Christ as a babe, was himself an Idumean, an Edomite thirsty for the blood of Israel's greatest Son (Isa. 9:6). Both historically and figuratively, Edom represents the enemy, all forms of opposition, to God's Church in general.

63.2-3 Wherefore art thou red in thine apparel, and

thy garments like him that treadeth in the winefat? 3 I have trodden the winepress alone; and of the people there was none with me: for I will tread them in mine anger, and trample them in my fury; and their blood shall be sprinkled upon my garments, and I will stain all my raiment.

63.2-3 The prophet asks rhetorically of the Lord, "Why are your clothes red as though you've been trending wine?" The King of Glory states emphatically that HE has cut off the wicked fruit from their vine and trodden out the grapes alone (Joel 3:13); HE is covered in red, the color of war, the blood of His enemies.

63.4. For the day of vengeance is in mine heart, and the year of my redeemed is come.

63.4 As the Lord spoke through Moses, He speaks through Isaiah; vengeance and recompense belong to the Lord alone (Deut. 32:35). This is His appointed day to avenge Himself of all His adversaries. (Jer. 46:10) Well does Isaiah remind us of the words of Amos; with fire will the Lord exact retribution upon Bozrah, a high city of Edom; for their persistent insolence He will not turn away from His punishment. (Amos 11:11-12)

63.5-6 And I looked, and there was none to help; and I wondered that there was none to uphold: therefore mine own arm brought salvation unto me; and my fury, it upheld me. 6 And I will tread down the people in mine anger, and make them drunk in my fury, and I will bring down their strength to the earth.

63.5-6 Unaided and without necessity of help, the Lord upholds Himself. Speaking both of an immediate rescue and reprisal for an exiled people, and concurrently for the eternal Church, the Lord will accomplish the task with His own Right Hand (Acts 5:30-31). We are reminded of. John's Revelation as the book is presented and none is found worthy to open it, save the Lion of Judah; He alone prevails to make ultimate judgment. (Rev. 5:1-5)

63.7-8 I will mention the lovingkindnesses of the Lord, and the praises of the Lord, according to all that the Lord hath bestowed on us, and the great goodness toward the house of Israel, which he hath bestowed on them according to his mercies, and according to the multitude of his lovingkindnesses. 8 For he said, Surely they are my people, children that will not lie: so he was their Saviour.

63.7-8 The tone here shifts from judgment to mercy, and the prophet calls to mind the words of King David, speaking of His "loving-kindness and tender mercies" towards Israel (Ps. 40:11, Ps. 51:1). He identifies with His people; He "knoweth them that are His." (Jer. 24:7; 2 Tim. 2:19)

63.9 In all their affliction he was afflicted, and the angel of his presence saved them: in his love and in his pity he redeemed them; and he bare them, and carried them all the days of old.

63.9 Throughout Israel's history, He has been with her, suffering affliction with her, grieving for her in the midst of necessary punishments (Ps. 22:24). Yet, for all that, He has never cast Israel away (Lev. 26:44). His promises are remembered and He has bourn Israel's iniquities; He has carried them always. (Is. 53:5)

63.10 But they rebelled, and vexed his holy Spirit: therefore he was turned to be their enemy, and he fought against them.

63.10 As from the emergence of a nation after Exodus, the rebellion of God's people exasperates his perfect spirit until judgment is required. The stiffening of necks necessitates a Heavenly response; disobedience to His will cannot persist unchecked by His judgment. (Deut. 9:6,13; Prov. 29:1; Acts 7:51)

63.11-15 Then he remembered the days of old, Moses, and his people, saying, Where is he that brought them up out of the sea with the shepherd of his flock? where is he that put his holy Spirit within him? 12 That led them by the right hand of Moses with his glorious arm, dividing the water before them, to make himself an everlasting name? 13 That led them through the deep, as an horse in the wilderness, that they should not stumble? 14 As a beast goeth down into the valley, the Spirit of the Lord caused him to rest: so didst thou lead thy people, to make thyself a glorious name. 15 Look down from heaven, and behold from the habitation of thy holiness and of thy glory: where is thy zeal and thy strength, the sounding of thy bowels and of thy mercies toward me? are they restrained?

63.11-15 At the height of their idolatry and exile, Isaiah speaks for the people as they remember the stories of old, how the Lord had saved them time and again (Ps. 106:43, 47). They know Him only in memory. They blindly grope for Him as Job did, looking forward, and to the past, but "cannot perceive Him" (Job 23:8).

63.16 Doubtless thou art our father, though Abraham

be ignorant of us, and Israel acknowledge us not: thou, O Lord, art our father, our redeemer; thy name is from everlasting.

63:16 The prophet proclaims that Abraham would assuredly renounce kinship with Israel because of their disobedience. As in the days that would come, though many things be supposedly done in His Name, The Lord searches the heart (Jer. 17:9-10) and will deny even knowing those who call upon Him yet oppose His will (Matt. 7:21-23).

63.17-19 O Lord, why hast thou made us to err from thy ways, and hardened our heart from thy fear? Return for thy servants' sake, the tribes of thine inheritance. 18 The people of thy holiness have possessed it but a little while: our adversaries have trodden down thy sanctuary. 19 We are thine: thou never barest rule over them; they were not called by thy name.

63.17-19 God will allow the heart that desires to be hardened to become so (Ex. 7:13-14). In that revelatory moment of contrition, the mind's eye of the people perceives, in hind sight, that they have possessed His promises for only a short time before He turned them over to the enemy. He has become without honor in His own country (Matt. 13:57), a stranger to His people (Jer. 14:8), as though He never ruled over them. The heart of Israel feels disinherited, as one He refuses to acknowledge as His own (Matt. 25:12, 41; John 10:14, 27).

Chapter 64

64.1-3 Oh that thou wouldest rend the heavens, that thou wouldest come down, that the mountains might flow down at thy presence, 2 As when the melting fire burneth, the fire causeth the waters to boil, to make thy name known to thine adversaries, that the nations may tremble at thy presence! 3 When thou didst terrible things which we looked not for, thou camest down, the mountains flowed down at thy presence.

64.1-3 In the opening words of chapter 64, we hear Isaiah, now serving as proxy for the voice of the people, crying out for a sign from God. As He did in the days of Moses, Isaiah desires to see God in fire and smoke on the mountain top (Ex. 19:11) in the sight of all the people. The prophet yearns for the Lord to rip open the Heavens and cause the mountain to quake as He once did (Ex. 19:18). Like the fire of God had once consumed the sacrifice of the altar (Lev. 9:24) the prophet longs for God to burn among the nations and cause them to bow to His igneous presence.

64.4 For since the beginning of the world men have not heard, nor perceived by the ear, neither hath the

eye seen, O God, beside thee, what he hath prepared for him that waiteth for him.

64:4 As Moses retold Israel's story and reinforced God'a law (Deut. 4:35), as Hannah worshipped childless and faithful (1 Sam. 2:2), as David prayed in humility following the words of Nathan the prophet (2. Sam. 7:22), Isaiah now speaks; surely, there is no other God like Him. The Apostle Paul takes his text for the Corinthian church directly from the prophet's words; our ears have not heard, nor have we perceived or seen with our eyes, all that He has prepared for those that serve Him faithfully (1 Cor. 2:9).

64.5-9 Thou meetest him that rejoiceth and worketh righteousness, those that remember thee in thy ways: behold, thou art wroth; for we have sinned: in those is continuance, and we shall be saved. 6 But we are all as an unclean thing, and all our righteousnesses are as filthy rags; and we all do fade as a leaf; and our iniquities, like the wind, have taken us away. 7 And there is none that calleth upon thy name, that stirreth up himself to take hold of thee: for thou hast hid thy face from us, and hast consumed us, because of our iniquities. 8 But now, O Lord, thou art our father; we are the clay, and thou our potter; and we all are the work of thy hand. 9 Be not wroth very sore, O Lord, neither remember iniquity for ever: behold, see, we beseech thee, we are all thy people.

64.5-9 Now is the whole admonition of wrongdoing laid upon the people, and a prayer made towards repentance. The Lord has been sure, but Israel has sinned. In the judgment of the man of God, on Israel's finest day her righteousness is no better than an old, filthy, tattered garment. Isaiah pleads with God to remember that He is Father to Israel, the Hands of the Potter's clay. With this expression of confession and obeisance there is a startling reminiscence of Nehemiah's words penned some two hundred and fifty years later in the court of Persia's King Artaxerxes; the grave acknowledgement of guilt seems inextricably bound to an eleventh-hour plea for redemption (Neh. 1:6-9).

64.10-12 Thy holy cities are a wilderness, Zion is a wilderness, Jerusalem a desolation. 11 Our holy and our beautiful house, where our fathers praised thee, is burned up with fire: and all our pleasant things are laid waste. 12 Wilt thou refrain thyself for these things, O Lord? wilt thou hold thy peace, and afflict us very sore?

64.10-12 In approximately 701 BC, Sennacherib, the king of Assyria, swept through the Kingdom of Judah, attacking its fortified cities, and laid siege to Jerusalem. In the remains of this war and desolated countryside the man of God asks God for an end to His silence, a resolution to the Lord holding back His hand of rescue.

Chapter 65

65.1-7 I am sought of them that asked not for me; I am found of them that sought me not: I said, Behold me, behold me, unto a nation that was not called by my name. 2 I have spread out my hands all the day unto a rebellious people, which walketh in a way that was not good, after their own thoughts; 3 A people that provoketh me to anger continually to my face; that sacrificeth in gardens, and burneth incense upon altars of brick; 4 Which remain among the graves, and lodge in the monuments, which eat swine's flesh, and broth of abominable things is in their vessels; 5 Which say, Stand by thyself, come not near to me; for I am holier than thou. These are a smoke in my nose, a fire that burneth all the day. 6 Behold, it is written before me: I will not keep silence, but will recompense, even recompense into their bosom, 7 Your iniquities, and the iniquities of your fathers together, saith the Lord, which have burned incense upon the mountains, and blasphemed me upon the hills: therefore will I measure their former work into their bosom.

65.1-7 Jehovah here responds to the prophet's questions. The Lord laments that, though He was ready to come to their aide, the people had not asked. He was ready to be found, but the heart of the nation sought its own self-contrived deliverances. Pagan ritual, incense to idols, worship of the dead, the eating of the unclean, and filthy self-righteousness have gone up as an acrid fume into His nostrils. In essence, all that has transpired has not come about because of a negligent thoughtlessness, but rather by His divine will for appointed judgment of their long-lived insolence.

65.8-10 Thus saith the Lord, As the new wine is found in the cluster, and one saith, Destroy it not; for a blessing is in it: so will I do for my servants' sakes, that I may not destroy them all. 9 And I will bring forth a seed out of Jacob, and out of Judah an inheritor of my mountains: and mine elect shall inherit it, and my servants shall dwell there. 10 And Sharon shall be a fold of flocks, and the valley of Achor a place for the herds to lie down in, for my people that have sought me.

65.8-10 Levitical Law always provided a remnant of the sacrifice as God's exclusively. So too does the Lord preserve a remnant of His people even at the height of their self-destructive behavior (Neh. 1:3, Ez. 6:8)

65.11-16 But ye are they that forsake the Lord, that forget my holy mountain, that prepare a table for that troop, and that furnish the drink offering unto that number. 12 Therefore will I number you to the sword, and ye shall all bow down to the slaughter: because when I called, ye did not answer; when I spake, ye did not hear; but did evil before mine eyes, and did choose that wherein I delighted not. 13 Therefore thus saith the Lord God, Behold, my servants shall eat, but ye shall be hungry: behold, my servants shall drink, but

ye shall be thirsty: behold, my servants shall rejoice, but ye shall be ashamed: 14 Behold, my servants shall sing for joy of heart, but ye shall cry for sorrow of heart, and shall howl for vexation of spirit. 15 And ye shall leave your name for a curse unto my chosen: for the Lord God shall slay thee, and call his servants by another name: 16 That he who blesseth himself in the earth shall bless himself in the God of truth; and he that sweareth in the earth shall swear by the God of truth; because the former troubles are forgotten, and because they are hid from mine eyes.

65.11-16 Never did God permit the ideas of luck, or chance, to be exalted above His supreme will in the canon set down by the hand of Moses. Because the people have clung to *"Fortune"* (troop: Hebrew-"Gad," meaning a distribution or chance) and *"Destiny"* (number: Hebrew-"Meni," meaning fate; a god of good luck) rather than His determination, He has "destined" them to go down by the edge of the blade. Now a juxtaposition is posed between the outcome of His servants and the ones who continually oppose Him. Like King David's "blessed man," those who attend upon the Lord will eat, drink, rejoice, and sing; but "the ungodly are not so" and will be hungry, thirsty, ashamed, sorrowful, and vexed. (Ps. 1:1-6)

65.17-20 For, behold, I create new heavens and a new earth: and the former shall not be remembered, nor come into mind. But be ye glad and rejoice for ever in that which I create: for, behold, I create Jerusalem a rejoicing, and her people a joy. 19 And I will rejoice in Jerusalem, and joy in my people: and the voice of weeping shall be no more heard in her, nor the voice of crying. 20 There shall be no more thence an infant of days, nor an old man that hath not filled his days: for the child shall die an hundred years old; but the sinner being an hundred years old shall be accursed.

65.17-20 The former things have passed away (2. Cor. 5:17) as God ushers in a new heaven and earth (Rev. 21:1-2). Again, with a gesture to the pressing return of exiles and an indication of perpetuity, these faithful are the "pillars" of. John's Temple (Rev. 3:12), those who have emerged victorious in a life lived for the Almighty. The Lord rejoices in His people and has "prepared them a place" (John 14:2) in the New Jerusalem. God will wipe away their tears and there will be "no more death, neither sorrow." be no more weeping or sorrow, but long life and joy (Luke 6:20-23).

65.21-23 And they shall build houses, and inhabit them; and they shall plant vineyards, and eat the fruit of them. 22 They shall not build, and another inhabit; they shall not plant, and another eat: for as the days of a tree are the days of my people, and mine elect shall long enjoy the work of their hands. 23 They shall not labour in vain, nor bring forth for trouble; for they are the seed of the blessed of the Lord, and their offspring with them.

65.21-23 The Lord will return His people and plant them in the land He gave. They will build houses; they will plant vineyards. Their days will be blessed, long, and their work not in vain (1.Cor. 15:58). Here is the promise to Abraham remembered and re-solidified; His seed will be blessed in the earth (Gen. 12:1-3).

65.24 And it shall come to pass, that before they call, I will answer; and while they are yet speaking, I will hear.

65.24 Here does the Lord promise a new thing to those who will turn to Him; "*before* they call" on Him, He will answer (Jer. 29:11-13). It is as if God is speaking through Isaiah in preparation, implanting the underlying concept of Calvary, for blood would be shed for all sin, even those sins *not yet* committed.

65.25 The wolf and the lamb shall feed together, and the lion shall eat straw like the bullock: and dust shall be the serpent's meat. They shall not hurt nor destroy in all my holy mountain, saith the Lord.

65.25 Isaiah leaves the reader of chapter 65 with the hope of Divinely appointed peace. The symbolic imagery of the wolf and lamb feeding together, the lion acting as a bullock, is itself an allusion to the coming Christ. He will be the embodiment of the Most Holy One. In that body He will carry all the superior qualities and excellent character traits of the One robed in flesh. He will be, at the same time, the Great Peacemaker, the "lamb slain before the foundation of the world" (Rev. 13:8), and He will be the Warrior for His people, the "lion of the tribe of Judah" (Rev. 5:5).

Chapter 66

66.1-2 Thus saith the Lord, The heaven is my throne, and the earth is my footstool: where is the house that ye build unto me? and where is the place of my rest? 2 For all those things hath mine hand made, and all those things have been, saith the Lord: but to this man will I look, even to him that is poor and of a contrite spirit, and trembleth at my word.

66.1-2 In much the same language used as in speaking to King David through Nathan the prophet (1. Sam. 7:5-7), the Lord confirms through Isaiah that there is no house made by human hands that can contain His Glory. The universe itself serves as His great throne of judgment and the earth provides a resting place for His feet. We may come close to His presence, not with the vain attempt of physical enshrinement, but exclusively through the heart of humility, the spirit of contrition. (Ps. 34:18, 51:17). One cannot approach Him without first trembling at His Word.

66.3-4 He that killeth an ox is as if he slew a man; he that sacrificeth a lamb, as if he cut off a dog's neck; he that offereth an oblation, as if he offered swine's blood; he that burneth incense, as if he blessed an idol.

Yea, they have chosen their own ways, and their soul delighteth in their abominations. 4 I also will choose their delusions, and will bring their fears upon them; because when I called, none did answer; when I spake, they did not hear: but they did evil before mine eyes, and chose that in which I delighted not.

66.3-4 Those who deliberately sin, that delight in the detestability of their own waywardness, are the enemy of His holiness and the focus of His vengeance.

66.5-14 Hear the word of the Lord, ye that tremble at his word; Your brethren that hated you, that cast you out for my name's sake, said, Let the Lord be glorified: but he shall appear to your joy, and they shall be ashamed. 6 A voice of noise from the city, a voice from the temple, a voice of the Lord that rendereth recompence to his enemies. 7 Before she travailed, she brought forth; before her pain came, she was delivered of a man child. 8 Who hath heard such a thing? who hath seen such things? Shall the earth be made to bring forth in one day? or shall a nation be born at once? for as soon as Zion travailed, she brought forth her children. 9 Shall I bring to the birth, and not cause to bring forth? saith the Lord: shall I cause to bring forth, and shut the womb? saith thy God. 10 Rejoice ye with Jerusalem, and be glad with her, all ye that love her: rejoice for joy with her, all ye that mourn for her: 11 That ye may suck, and be satisfied with the breasts of her consolations; that ye may milk out, and be delighted with the abundance of her glory. 12 For thus saith the Lord, Behold, I will extend peace to her like a river, and the glory of the Gentiles like a flowing stream: then shall ye suck, ye shall be borne upon her sides, and be dandled upon her knees. 13 As one whom his mother comforteth, so will I comfort you; and ye shall be comforted in Jerusalem. 14 And when ye see this, your heart shall rejoice, and your bones shall flourish like an herb: and the hand of the Lord shall be known toward his servants, and his indignation toward his enemies.

66.5-14 God's people, those faithful which once heard nothing but the voice of rejection from their brethren, now hear the "roar" of vengeance from the Lion of Judah out of Holy Zion (Joel 3:16; Amos 1:2). Presently Zion, without pain or travel, will, in a moment, restore the land full of men lost to war and exile; but for a bright future yet to come, she will bring forth her Redeeming Son (Is. 9:6). As Jochebed delivered 600,000 children to the light of freedom *in one day* by bringing forth Moses (Ex. 6:20; Nu. 26:59), so too will Zion bear the deliverer of all mankind. Zion is the woman of the sun in Revelation 12 and she will bring forth that Great Shepherd who ushers in Heaven to earth. He will be flowing rivers of living water (John 7:38), the "riches of the glory of this mystery" preached to the Gentiles (Col. 1:27; 1 Tim. 3:16).

66.15-19 For, behold, the Lord will come with fire, and with his chariots like a whirlwind, to render his anger with fury, and his rebuke with flames of fire. 16 For by fire and by his sword will the Lord plead with all flesh: and the slain of the Lord shall be many. 17 They that sanctify themselves, and purify themselves in the gardens behind one tree in the midst, eating swine's flesh, and the abomination, and the mouse, shall be consumed together, saith the Lord. 18 For I know their works and their thoughts: it shall come, that I will gather all nations and tongues; and they

shall come, and see my glory. 19 And I will set a sign among them, and I will send those that escape of them unto the nations, to Tarshish, Pul, and Lud, that draw the bow, to Tubal, and Javan, to the isles afar off, that have not heard my fame, neither have seen my glory; and they shall declare my glory among the Gentiles.

66.15-19 Now is the fierceness of his vengeance pronounced (Ps. 18:8-9, 13; Is. 30:27), the implement by which He judges the earth and ushers in eternity. He is all consuming fire (Rev. 1:14), He is that "faithful and true" who makes war to end all war (Rev. 19:11-12). He comes to judge the profane who would eat the unclean (Lev. 11:29), the idolatrous who would worship the forbidden (Lev. 26:1; Deut. 16:21), and the self-righteous (condemned in Matthew 23). As the Jews would seek a sign and the Greeks wisdom (1. Cor. 1:22) it is promised to be given (Rev. 12:1); those that the Lord will spare will be used to spread the wonder ("sign") of His fame (Ex. 10:2) among the Gentile world (Rom. 15:16).

66.20-24 And they shall bring all your brethren for an offering unto the Lord out of all nations upon horses, and in chariots, and in litters, and upon mules, and upon swift beasts, to my holy mountain Jerusalem, saith the Lord, as the children of Israel bring an offering in a clean vessel into the house of the Lord. 21 And I will also take of them for priests and for Levites, saith the Lord. 22 For as the new heavens and the new earth, which I will make, shall remain before me, saith the Lord, so shall your seed and your name remain. 23 And it shall come to pass, that from one new moon to another, and from one sabbath to another, shall all flesh come to worship before me, saith the Lord. 24 And they shall go forth, and look

upon the carcases of the men that have transgressed against me: for their worm shall not die, neither shall their fire be quenched; and they shall be an abhorring unto all flesh.

66.20-24 Israel will return to her homeland (Is. 49:12; Jer. 30:3-4; Eze. 38:8) and from among the ranks of the once fatherless Gentiles (John 14:18, "*comfortless*" is the Greek: "*ophanos*" - meaning orphans) He will take a holy priesthood sanctified to Himself (1 Pet. 2:5,9; Rev. 1:5-6; Rev. 5:9-10). Those who overcome shall not have their names blotted out from the Lamb's Book of Life (Deut. 29:20; 2 Kings 14: 27; Jer. 5:18 Rev. 3:5) and. those that obey will have their seed forever blessed (Gen. 22:18; Gen. 26:4). Walking hand in hand with the promise of eternal life, to those who will follow Him, is the guarantee that those who, in themselves, cause offense to Him (Mark 9:43-48) will have everlasting judgment. The worm (signifying decay) will never cease and the fire (designating a purifying destruction) will never go out.

www.ingramcontent.com/pod-product-compliance
Lightning Source LLC
Chambersburg PA
CBHW071728080526
44588CB00013B/1934